WHAT YOUR COLLEAGUES ARE SAYING . .

"*Teaching Students to Drive Their Learning* is a timely playbook that the research and tools to support student agency in learning. Seamless research-based practices into clear actions that teachers can quickly impler. classrooms, this book is a must-read for all."

—Arlena Gaynor, Executive Director of Language, Literacy, and Social Studies, Dallas ISD

"The newest Corwin playbook is one that should be in the library of every educator who strives to accelerate the learning of their students. Through clever analogies and real-world examples, this book creates a clear path paved with strategies for teaching students to take ownership of their own learning and become life-long learners who seek challenges and thrive on their own growth. It's a practical guide to developing the qualities of self-driven learners in your students and promoting a classroom culture that allows the teacher to confidently let students take on challenges and effectively become their own teachers."

—Jessica Javo, Instructional Supervisor/Assistant Principal South Effingham Elementary School

"This is a great read for all educators! It really speaks to how we, as educators, need to help students become responsible for their own learning. Students truly need to know what to do when they don't know what to do!"

—Lydia Bagley, Instructional Support Specialist Cobb County School District

"This playbook is a great refresher for experienced teachers on ways that they can support students who are having difficulty finding success in the classroom. It's a gentle nod and a great reminder of best practices that all teachers can benefit from."

—Melissa Black, Elementary Educator and Education Consultant

"Since implementing Visible Learning practices, we have made great strides as a school district. We have embedded the use of learning intentions and success criteria in our classrooms and made them visible, utilizing them to guide instruction and referencing them as the basis for assessment and reflection. Our students now understand what they are learning, how they know when they've learned it, and where they need to go next."

—Katie Isch, Principal, Adams Central Community School

TEACHING STUDENTS TO DRIVE THEIR LEARNING

GRADES K–12

TEACHING STUDENTS TO DRIVE THEIR LEARNING

A PLAYBOOK ON ENGAGEMENT AND SELF-REGULATION

GRADES K–12

DOUGLAS FISHER
NANCY FREY
SARAH ORTEGA
JOHN HATTIE

CORWIN

FOR INFORMATION:

Corwin

A SAGE Company

2455 Teller Road

Thousand Oaks, California 91320

(800) 233-9936

www.corwin.com

SAGE Publications Ltd.

1 Oliver's Yard

55 City Road

London EC1Y 1SP

United Kingdom

SAGE Publications India Pvt. Ltd.

Unit No 323-333, Third Floor, F-Block

International Trade Tower Nehru Place

New Delhi 110 019

India

SAGE Publications Asia-Pacific Pte. Ltd.

18 Cross Street #10-10/11/12

China Square Central

Singapore 048423

President: Mike Soules

Vice President and Editorial
  Director: Monica Eckman

Director and Publisher,
  Corwin Classroom: Lisa Luedeke

Associate Content
  Development Editor: Sarah Ross

Production Editor: Melanie Birdsall

Copy Editor: Cate Huisman

Typesetter: C&M Digitals (P) Ltd.

Proofreader: Jeff Bryant

Cover Designer: Janet Kiesel

Marketing Manager: Megan Naidl

Printed in the United Kingdom

ISBN 9781071918951

Library of Congress Control Number: 2023936473

This book is printed on acid-free paper.

23 24 25 26 27 10 9 8 7 6 5 4 3 2 1

CONTENTS

Visit the companion website at
resources.corwin.com/teachingstudentstodrivetheirlearning
for downloadable resources.

ACKNOWLEDGMENTS

Corwin gratefully acknowledges the contributions of the following reviewers:

Lydia Bagley
Instructional Support Specialist
Cobb County School District

Melissa Black
Elementary Educator and Education Consultant
District of Columbia Public Schools

Tiffany S. Coleman
Instructional Coach
Baggett Elementary School

Ruthanne Munger
Writing Specialist, Grades K–12
Union School Corporation

INTRODUCTION

This book is about student engagement and self-regulation, but it's not about bribes and control. Rather, it's about designing experiences that allow students to learn more and better. The phrase we use to convey this idea is "teaching students to drive their learning." Teachers play a critical role in creating the conditions that allow students to do so. This playbook is designed for you to work with as you validate and extend what you know. You may choose to jump around, engaging with different modules based on what you or your team need at the time. Or you may decide to read the modules in order. You'll note that the first module sets the stage by focusing on engagement. We propose that high levels of engagement require specific actions and thinking from students and changes in classroom procedures and experiences. When students successfully reach high levels of engagement, they're not simply compliant. Instead, they drive their learning.

> Who wouldn't want students to be leaders of their learning, to be engaged in learning tasks, and to take responsibility?

Following this opening module, we focus on the six factors that allow students to drive their learning (see Figure i.1). You'll note that there are many interactive features designed for you to engage more fully with the ideas in each module. We hope you, and perhaps your team, will try on these tools and make this playbook your own. In the final module, we focus on the reasons that students disengage, and we present nine cognitive challenges, and what educators can do about them, to return students to the driver's seat of their learning. But first, let's meet a real student from San Diego who exemplifies the characteristics of students who drive their learning.

Figure i.1 Characteristics of Students Who Drive Their Learning

Assessment-capable learners

1. Know their current level of understanding
2. Know where they are going and they are confident to take on the challenge
3. Select tools to guide their learning
4. Seek feedback and recognize that errors are opportunities to learn
5. Monitor their progress and adjust their learning
6. Recognize their learning and teach others

MEET QUINN

Quinn had a history of struggle in school and, in fact, was recommended by a previous school for grade-level retention. Quinn's mom knew that simply repeating the same class with the same content was not the answer for her child. She transferred Quinn to a different school, one that was focused on teaching students to become responsible for their learning. Two years later, Quinn is performing nearly at grade level. Quinn is also much happier and more engaged with peers, learning, and school work.

The difference? Quinn and classmates have learned how to drive their learning. The idea is appealing, isn't it? Who wouldn't want students to be leaders of their learning, engage in learning tasks, and take responsibility for teaching themselves and others? But what does it mean to have students drive their learning? Let's review the experiences that Quinn has had.

On a daily basis, Quinn can tell you what the class is learning. Quinn also understands what current levels of learning mean, recognizing that there is no "bad" place to be. Quinn can identify "I know where I'm going," which is one of the signature characteristics of students who drive their learning. Perhaps more importantly, Quinn knows what to do next to further learning. The tasks teachers assign allow Quinn to engage in learning that is just the right amount of challenging—not too easy, not too hard, and not too boring.

Quinn also can select the tools needed for the journey. For example, while working on an essay, Quinn recalled prior lessons that focused on writing introductions and chose an introduction type to match the topic. On another day, Quinn asked for peer feedback on a draft, recognizing this type of support provides another learning opportunity. Quinn's teachers have taught a range of cognitive and meta-cognitive tools, but it is up to Quinn to select from them and then apply them to the learning task.

> Students often wrongly believe that errors are evidence of their character, rather than an expected and welcome part of learning.

Quinn also has come to understand *what to do when you don't know what to do.* That sounds complex, but it is straightforward. When Quinn gets stuck, there are strategies in place to help get unstuck. For example, when confronted with a complex mathematical task, Quinn was not sure where to start. Rather than be stymied by this, Quinn decided to reread the problem and identify the given and the units, ask what the problem was asking, and check with a peer to validate thinking. Quinn could also seek help from teachers and peers, work backward from the answer to better understand the math ideas and steps, or rework some of the basic math ideas inherent in the task. Quinn struggled with this task but knows that there are actions that can be taken to figure out things.

Quinn also engages in self-talk, recognizing that there are things to do to become successful in the face of setbacks or when learning progress stalls. Quinn knows that a wide range of supports—teacher and peers—is available to ensure success. In other words, Quinn is beginning to see errors are opportunities for learning. This is key, as students often wrongly believe that errors are evidence of their character, rather than an expected and welcome part of learning. Errors should never be seen as sources of embarrassment or statements about one's skills and commitment, but as wonderful opportunities to tackle the next most appropriate challenges. In Quinn's school, teachers regularly comment, "We celebrate errors because they're opportunities to learn." They teach their students how to recognize their own errors. Then these teachers leverage these errors for the learner's benefit.

Further, Quinn knows how to track progress. Of course, the teachers also monitor progress through formative evaluation of students' work and summative tasks that allow them to demonstrate mastery. But Quinn knows that responsibility is shared with the teacher, and they can monitor learning together. Quinn does not wait for feedback from others but instead seeks out feedback from peers and the teacher.

In addition, Quinn has been taught several strategies to self-assess. For example, the teachers have provided students with a checklist for assessing their own participation within the group (see Figure i.2). Quinn has come to appreciate that quality engagement with peers directly affects their collective learning. Quinn and the teachers know that learning is enhanced when students are active participants in the discussion. Quinn has discovered several skills, including getting the group back on track when they lose focus.

Figure i.2   Self-Assessment for Collaborative Learning

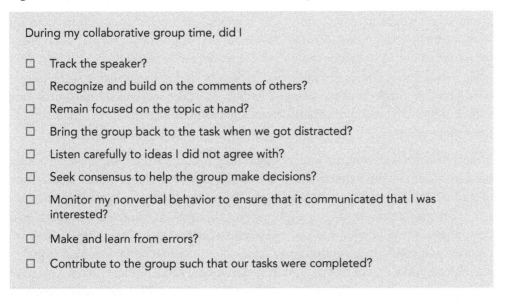

During my collaborative group time, did I

☐   Track the speaker?

☐   Recognize and build on the comments of others?

☐   Remain focused on the topic at hand?

☐   Bring the group back to the task when we got distracted?

☐   Listen carefully to ideas I did not agree with?

☐   Seek consensus to help the group make decisions?

☐   Monitor my nonverbal behavior to ensure that it communicated that I was interested?

☐   Make and learn from errors?

☐   Contribute to the group such that our tasks were completed?

online resources Available for download at **resources.corwin.com/teachingstudentstodrivetheirlearning**

And finally, Quinn recognizes when learning has occurred and engages in teaching others. The best exit ticket from any series of lessons is the skill to then teach others. This implies confidence in knowing and understanding what has been taught. As teachers, we know that we need to listen to others, evaluate how they are solving problems, and teach them to monitor their progress—the very skills we also want to develop in our students. While monitoring success, Quinn notes where those successes lie and which areas still require attention. Quinn communicates this with teachers (and others, including family members), working to interpret learning data and setting mastery goals. Quinn knows that learning is important and is motivated by success. This success drives Quinn to want to learn more, and the cycle starts again. As a result, Quinn is engaged in learning and uses a number of self-regulation strategies. No one had to tell Quinn to be engaged; rather, teachers focused on teaching all students in the school to drive their learning.

For many people, this sounds idealistic and unattainable. But it did happen. It happened for Quinn, a real student in a real school, with real teachers who understood the value of teaching students to drive their learning. Those teachers provided Quinn and others with specific experiences that built their competence and confidence, reinforcing the necessary characteristics that learners who self-regulate and take responsibility for their own learning possess. It's not pie in the sky but an attainable goal when school teams focus on a few things that work well. And it is not just students who learn to think this way. Their teachers also think about their role to teach students to think, act, and become their own teachers—to know what to do when they do not know what to do. We introduced you to Quinn to show you it's possible. If you aspire to have students drive their learning, each of the factors explored above is critical to success. And the foundation for this is Visible Learning®.

WHAT IS VISIBLE LEARNING?

Visible Learning describes a constellation of efforts. It is a research database (see Meta[x], **www.visiblelearningmetax.com**), a school improvement initiative (see https://us.corwin.com/en-us/nam/visible-learning), and a call to action to focus on what works best to impact learning (Hattie, 2023). The *Visible Learning* database is composed of over 2,100 meta-analyses of the work of over 400 million students. That is big data when it comes to education. In fact, some have said that it is the largest educational research database amassed to date. To make sense of so much data, one author of this playbook, John Hattie, focuses his work on interpreting the meaning of these meta-analyses.

A meta-analysis is a statistical tool for combining findings from different studies with the goal of identifying patterns that can inform practice. In other words, it is a study of studies. The tool that is used to aggregate the information is an *effect size.* An effect size is the magnitude, or size, of a given effect. To draw an imperfect but functional comparison, consider what you know about how earthquakes are measured. They are reported as an order of magnitude on a scale called a Richter scale. Some earthquakes are imperceptible except by specialized measurement tools. Other earthquakes have a minimal "shake" that results in a small, momentary impact but no lasting effects. A few register high on the Richter scale and have a definitive impact on an area. Just as numbers on the Richter scale help us understand the effect of an earthquake, effect sizes from meta-analyses of several studies help us understand the impact of an educational influence.

> Understanding the effect size lets teachers know how powerful a given influence is in changing achievement.

For example, imagine a study that demonstrated statistically significant findings ($p < 0.01$ for example) for having students stand while learning math. People might buy stock in "standing tables," and a new teaching fad would be born. But then suppose, upon deeper reading, you learned that the students who stood had a 0.02 month gain (an effect size of 0.02) over the control group, an effect size pretty close to zero. You realize that the results were statistically significant because the sample size was large, but the size of the learning gain itself was not very meaningful. Would you still buy standing desks and demand that students stand while learning math? Probably not (and we made this example up, anyway).

Meta-analyses can also identify whether an overall effect size differs across contexts. For example, is it different in elementary school versus high school, for males and females, in San Diego or Melbourne? Understanding the effect size lets us know how powerful a given influence is in changing achievement—in other words, the impact for the effort. Some things are hard to implement and have very little impact. Other things are easy to implement and still have limited impact. Educators search for things that have a greater impact, some of which will be harder to implement and some of which will be easier to put into play. When deciding what to implement to positively impact students' learning, wouldn't you like to know what the effect size is going forward? Then you can decide if it's worth the effort.

John was able to demonstrate that influences, strategies, actions, and so on with an effect size greater than 0.40 allow students to learn at an appropriate rate, meaning at least a year of growth for a year in school. While it provides an overall average, often specific conditions can be more critical—such as whether you are measuring a narrow construct (like vocabulary words known) or a wider construct (such as creative thinking). Before this level was established, teachers and researchers did not have a way to determine an acceptable threshold. Thus, weak practices, often supported with statistically significant studies, continued.

Let's consider some real examples from the Visible Learning database (www.visible learningmetax.com). We'll focus on a few factors that we think of as prerequisites for teaching students to drive their learning.

TEACHER EXPECTATIONS

All teachers have expectations for their students. Therefore, there really is no point in asking the question, "Do teachers have expectations for their students?" The better question is, "Do they have false and misleading expectations that lead to decrements in learning or learning gains—and for which students?" (Hattie, 2023, p. 220). The effect size of teachers' expectations for student learning is 0.58. Let's state it another way: If teachers expect their students to learn a full year (or more) of content for a year of input, they probably will. These expectations are communicated every day, in ways that include everything from the teacher's demeanor to the challenge of tasks assigned to students. Expectations must be at the forefront as teachers plan units of study and engage students in quality learning experiences. (Sadly, if teachers expect students will not make a full year's growth, they probably will not, regardless of the student's potential, interests, prior achievement, etc.)

TEACHER CREDIBILITY

Learning is a risk-taking endeavor. It requires that the learners put their faith in the teacher's ability to lead. The credibility of the teacher inspires confidence and a willingness to be open to risk. It is also a source of motivation for students to draw on when the learning is difficult or when a setback occurs. Being able to tell oneself, "I know my teachers know what they're doing, so I'll be okay" speaks to the trust the student has in the teacher.

The teacher's credibility inspires confidence and increases the students' willingness to be open to risk.

Teacher credibility involves three constructs: "competence, character (or trustworthiness), and perceived caring" (Finn et al., 2009, p. 519). The first, competence, is related to the teacher's projected subject matter knowledge and ability to organize instruction. (Nancy recalls her six-year-old granddaughter's assessment of a substitute teacher's first day: "Nana, she doesn't know the right math!") The second construct, which is character, includes perceptions of fairness and respect. (John recalls one of his sons saying that a teacher "treated everyone the same." When asked how, John's son said, "It's not like we all get the same rewards or punishments regardless of what we do; there is no fairness in that.") The third, which is caring, is understood by students to include responsiveness and nonverbal actions such as eye contact, smiling, and open and inviting body language. Doug recalls a professor of his who said, "I don't know how you're going to learn this, but it's on the midterm." The effect size of teacher credibility is 1.09, and it is simple: If a teacher is not perceived as credible, the students just turn off.

We chose these effects because they clearly impact students' learning and are not likely to be a surprise to educators. There is sufficient evidence to back up the claim that these three factors increase students' likelihood of learning. We'll focus on a number of effect sizes throughout this playbook and provide the magnitude of the effect for each. Of course, you can look up all of the effects—positive, neutral, and negative—on the website (www.visiblelearningmetax.com), but this playbook is about putting them into action so that students take responsibility for their own learning.

CONCLUSION

We have a goal for schools to make learning visible to every student. That's a tall order. It requires that teachers focus more on learning and less on teaching. Yes, we all use a range of instructional approaches, but is this instruction resulting in learning? That means we must know the impact we have on learning; we measure it and monitor it. And teach the students to monitor and evaluate their own progress, their strategies of learning, and their closeness to the success criteria for the lesson(s).

In order to make learning visible, we must teach students to drive their learning. Too many students are adult-dependent learners. Others are compliant learners. Too many teachers have no concept of "release of responsibility" (Fisher & Frey, 2021). Too many students (especially the above-average students) want the teacher to provide all the direction, as these students like direction and are good at following it, and it is easier for them to comply with teacher direction than to direct their own learning. Still others avoid learning altogether. Neither approach will serve our society well. What we need are learners who understand their current performance, recognize the gap between their current performance and the expected performance, and select strategies to close that gap. When schools are filled with students who have those characteristics, learning becomes not only visible but also palpable. In that case, as students become drivers of their learning and assume shared responsibility for their learning, learning is not limited to experiences inside the classroom.

What we need are learners who understand their current performance, recognize the gap between their current performance and the expected performance, and select strategies to close that gap.

1

ENGAGEMENT
From Disrupting to Driving Learning

LEARNING INTENTION

We are learning about engagement and the ways in which we can teach students to drive their learning.

SUCCESS CRITERIA

- I can discuss the value of viewing engagement as a continuum.

- I can describe each of the levels of engagement and identify student actions at each level.

- I can identify factors that allow students to drive their learning.

Educators know how important engagement is for student learning, but do we ever teach it? Caring and responsive educators recognize the fundamental importance of acquiring the academic skills and accompanying language needed to succeed in subject areas and therefore teach both with intention. Yet curiously, we often leave investment in their own engagement almost entirely up to the students. Instead, there is an overreliance on external mechanisms, including classroom rules and extrinsic rewards like table points, but little in the way of instruction on engagement. This puts students at heightened risk for the punitive measures of punishment and exclusion. We'll put it another way: When school is viewed as a series of compliance hoops to jump through, rather than a place of learning and mutual investment, we all lose.

------------------------------•
Students engage
when they learn to
drive their learning.

Nearly every student has a deep reservoir of motivation, but many choose not to invest their motivation in school work. So often the disengaged in class are absorbed with nonschool tasks (videos, social life, sport, music, etc.). Engagement is not a function of pushing and pulling students to do the work and love the subject, but an argument as to why they should invest in this work rather than that work.

But we all want to win. In fact, we want to create win-win situations in which students learn more and better, and their teachers recognize the impact of these situations on students. In the previous paragraph, we made it seem simple: *teach engagement*. And we do believe that students should understand what it means to engage in learning. But it's more complicated than that. As we will explore in this module, there are levels of engagement. Simply participating in class is not sufficient to ensure deep learning, much less assuming responsibility for your own learning. We see engagement as much more comprehensive and expansive. We won't bury the lede: *Students engage when they learn to drive their learning.* The question is, how do we create the conditions necessary for students to do so? What needs to occur for students to take increased responsibility for their learning, self-regulate their actions, and take ownership of their progress? That's true engagement. And that's the focus of this playbook.

TEXT IMPRESSION STRATEGY

The Text Impression strategy is used to activate a learner's background knowledge and invite predictions about a topic (McGinley & Denner, 1987). It uses a list of vocabulary words and phrases directly from the text. Learners use the list to write their own summary of the text before they have read it. They later compare their initial text impression with what they learn when they read the text. Text Impressions increase curiosity about the text and invite readers to engage more deeply in what they are reading. Importantly, curiosity has an effect size of 0.90, with a strong potential to accelerate learning. In each of the modules that follow, we'll invite you to engage in the Text Impression strategy.

TEXT IMPRESSION

Use the following words (in any order that works for you) to create an impression about what you think will be covered in this module.

behavioral engagement • cognitive engagement • emotional engagement • continuum • investing • withdrawing • engagement intention

_____

_____

_____

_____

_____

_____

_____

_____

_____

_____

_____

_____

_____

Engagement is at the core of learning (Eccles & Wang, 2012). Disengaged students learn less and are often negatively labeled as "unmotivated" or having "a behavior problem." Without question, a disengaged learner may well be a bored one. With an effect size of −0.46, boredom is a powerful decelerator to student learning. Many of us have witnessed this firsthand, as students put their hoodies up and their heads down. Or they turn their attention to something else such as a device or peer rather than the learning at hand.

Gauging student engagement is more than just cataloging who is turning in their assignments or leaning forward in their seats with eyes on the teacher. Engagement has historically been understood across three dimensions: behavioral, cognitive, and emotional (Fredricks et al., 2004). But these three dimensions are so interrelated that none of them is individually very predictive of student success. Of course, if a student is sleeping, they can't engage. And if students are asking relevant questions, they are more likely to be engaged. Following a review of a historical model of engagement, we'll turn to a model that presents engagement along a continuum, which we find more compelling from a learning perspective.

Berry (2020, 2022) took a novel approach to this engagement conundrum by asking teachers how these dimensions were manifested by their students. These interviews revealed that teachers saw engagement as a continuum of passive and active forms of engagement as well as disengagement. Instead of seeing engagement as a dichotomy—students are engaged or not—the continuum suggests that there is a range of actions, which can include a mixture of the cognitive, metacognitive, behavioral, and emotional dimensions that result in a state of being during learning. Berry called these stages of engagement *disrupting, avoiding, withdrawing, participating, investing,* and *driving.*

Since Berry's studies were published, classroom teachers around the world have utilized the continuum of engagement as a toehold for teaching students about its role in learning. Using the continuum as a visual, they name and label each stage of engagement, equipping their students with the behavioral, cognitive, and emotional language to take ownership of their learning by setting their goals and intentions. In other words, they teach the tools of self-regulation that are essential inside and outside of school. There are different ways that teachers help students to set their engagement intention and monitor their levels of engagement. Here are a few examples:

- A kindergarten teacher developed a graphic version of the continuum and placed it on each student's desk. Students placed a chip on the image that matched their intention and then were asked to self-assess at the end of the lesson.

- A third-grade teacher had students create posters for each stage. At various times during the day, students moved their nameplates to one of the posters to indicate their intention for that time period.

- A sixth-grade teacher gave each student a die and had them turn a number up to represent which stage they intended to be at, ranging from 1 for disrupting to 6 for driving.

- A middle school math teacher had index cards printed with labels for each stage. Each student was given a set of six cards on a ring. They could choose the card for the stage they were at and place it on top of their desk.

- A high school science teacher had students indicate their intention through the quiz feature in their learning management system. At the start of each period, students responded to the "quiz" so that the teacher would know where each student intended to be.

As noted in these examples, there is not just one way to invite students to set their engagement intention. But each of these ways allowed students to recognize their internal state of mind and communicate it with their teacher. A middle school teacher told us,

> Having students set their intention for engagement helps me make adjustments to the learning. And it helps me make decisions about how I approach different learners. For example, if a student tells me that they are withdrawn, it invites a conversation so that I can figure out what's happening and if there are things that I need to do because of that. When students are clear about their level of engagement, I take some of their actions less personally, which keeps me focused on the learning.

As Dewey noted many years ago, "We do not learn from experience. We learn from reflecting on experience. Reliving of an experience leads to making connections between information and feelings produced by the experience" (Dewey, 1933, p. 78). The essence of successful reflection is making evaluative claims—was the experience worthwhile, and did it have a positive impact on learning?

PAUSE AND PONDER

What is your reflection about teaching students about engagement?

_____
_____
_____
_____
_____
_____
_____
_____
_____
_____

How might you have students set their engagement intention and then reflect on their level of engagement?

_____
_____
_____
_____
_____
_____
_____
_____
_____
_____
_____

EXPLORING THE CONTINUUM OF ENGAGEMENT

Notice that the continuum locates passive thinking and actions in the center and radiates in both directions as students become more active. And yes, we've all seen students who are actively disengaged as well as those who were actively engaged. As we have noted, teaching students the language of engagement is helpful, but getting students to drive their learning is more complicated than simply labeling the stages. We'll consider each of the stages with notes about students who exhibited specific actions.

> Many of the students who disrupt learning are actually struggling academically and would rather be seen as "the bad kid" than as "the stupid kid."

Disrupting Learning

In this case, students are actively disengaged, and their behavioral and cognitive actions indicate that they are not learning. They may be engaged in problematic behaviors, including actions that harm others. They may also yell out in class, make jokes, and generally cause a scene. In terms of their cognitive and metacognitive engagement, they are not in the learning space. Their attention is elsewhere and may even be devious or destructive. Interestingly, many students who disrupt learning are struggling academically and would rather be seen as "the bad kid" than "the stupid kid." We're not excusing the behavior; teachers need systems to interrupt the disruption, such as restorative practices and positive behavioral support systems. But we all recognize that disrupting learning means that there is likely very little learning occurring.

Avoiding Learning

Although they are not disrupting the learning of others, students at this stage along the continuum are avoiding tasks that allow them to learn. They are often off task but may be doing things that seem useful, such as sharpening a pencil or waiting for help. Of course, both of those can be useful in the right context, but often they are signs that the student is avoiding learning. They may also be off task doing things that are counterproductive to their learning, such as playing video games on their phone or leaving for the restroom when they don't really need to go. When the cognitive demands are too great, learners may need a break and may seem, at least temporarily, as if they are avoiding learning.

The ultimate avoidance behavior is absenteeism. At a time in education when we are witnessing unprecedented levels of this, we must be courageous enough to look into the "black box of chronic absenteeism" that includes student well-being and the learning climate (Childs & Lofton, 2021, p. 215). Unfortunately, these are not commonly considered when examining the root causes that lead some students to vote with their feet by not showing up at all. The key is whether or not students (and schools) have the tools necessary to recognize that they are avoiding learning and then to change this behavior.

Withdrawing From Learning

Sometimes, students withdraw more passively from learning and learning tasks, physically or cognitively. In some cases, students remove themselves from their peers to withdraw from learning, and other times they stare into space, put their headphones on, or hide their faces. The good thing is that they are not distracting others. The bad thing is that they are not learning. Cognitively, these students may not see relevance in the learning goals, or they may not have sufficient prior knowledge to make sense of the current learning.

> Unfortunately, sometimes we accept participation as engagement and don't expect much more.

Participating in Learning

The first level on the engagement side of the continuum is still fairly passive. Unfortunately, sometimes we accept participating as engagement and don't expect much more. After all, the student is doing the work and seems to be paying attention. Frankly, that is a pretty low bar, and it confuses compliance with learning. When students get to this stage, they're much more likely to learn some things than when they withdraw, avoid, or disrupt learning. However, they will not learn to drive their learning or take responsibility for their learning at this stage. It's just too passive, and we shouldn't accept this as sufficient engagement but rather teach students the behavioral, cognitive, and emotional actions that allow them to invest in and drive their learning.

Investing in Learning

This is when students begin to take increased responsibility for their own learning. It's not just about doing work, but rather about valuing the learning. At this phase, students are much more curious and ask more questions. They engage with their peers and talk about what they are learning with others. In fact, they are excited about learning and anticipate future learning. Behaviorally, they are much more attentive and think along with their teachers, rather than observe their teachers doing the work.

Driving Learning

The highest level of engagement is reserved for students who drive their learning. Yes, they complete tasks and pay attention. They ask questions and think along with their teachers. But they take this to the next level as they set goals for themselves based on the class's learning intentions. They seek feedback from others and monitor their progress, often using tools their teachers have provided. They are so invested in their learning that they teach others, because they see that learning is valuable.

We have created a graphic version of this continuum with some of the actions that students take at each stage (see Figure 1.1).

Figure 1.1 A Continuum of Engagement

ACTIVE ◄─────────────── PASSIVE ───────────────► ACTIVE

Disrupting	Avoiding	Withdrawing	Participating	Investing	Driving
Distracting others	Looking for ways to avoid work	Being distracted	Doing work	Asking questions	Setting goals for themselves based on what the class is learning
Disrupting the learning environment	Off-task behaviors	Physically separating from group	Paying attention	Valuing the learning	
Engaging in problematic behavior	Packing backpack before class ends	Daydreaming	Responding to questions	Recognizing that there are things worth learning	Seeking feedback from others
Destruction of materials	Using various excuses to leave the classroom	Sleeping in class	Observing teachers doing work	Collaborating with peers	Self-assessing and monitoring progress
Persistent talking about something other than the topic of the lesson	Returning to class late from a break	Acting or imitating participation	Following teacher instructions	Talking about their learning with others	Teaching others
Speaking with unkind words		Hyperfocus on a task other than the one at hand	Complying with a new rule	Thinking along with their teachers	Being inspired to learn more about a topic or pursue an interest

DISENGAGEMENT | | | **ENGAGEMENT**

Source: Adapted from the work of Berry (2022).

Wouldn't it be great if all it took to engage students and significantly impact their learning was to show them the continuum of engagement?? As every educator knows, it's not that simple. Yes, students should know what it means to engage, but they deserve to be taught what it means to drive their learning. Doing so is a daily exercise, one that requires shifts in the experiences that students have. To be clear, we believe that teachers also have responsibilities in the classroom, and they should help students drive their learning. We are not suggesting that educators abdicate their responsibilities in the name of students driving their learning. Teachers are a significant variable in students' learning, but it's what the teachers do that makes the difference.

To make recommendations about teaching students to drive their learning, we draw on the work of Absolum et al. (2009), Conley and French (2014), Frey et al. (2018), and a host of learning sciences and educational psychology research (cited in each of the modules in this playbook). We have organized the research evidence and our experiences into factors that guide experiences for students to learn to drive their learning, including the following:

- **I know where I'm going**. Students understand their current performance and how it relates to the learning intention and success criteria, as well as the longer learning progressions.

- **I have the tools for the journey**. Students understand that they can select from a range of strategies to move their learning forward, especially when progress is interrupted.

- **I monitor my progress**. Students seek and respond to feedback from others, including peers and teachers, as they assess their own performance. Students know that making mistakes is expected in learning and indicates an opportunity for further learning.

- **I recognize when I'm ready for what's next**. Students interpret their data in light of the learning intention and success criteria of the lessons, as well as the overall learning progression, to identify when they are ready to move on.

- **I know what to do next**. Knowing what to do *when you do not know what to do* is surely the mark of the educated person. It is the difference between knowing how to persist and simply giving up when faced with an early challenge. It is the essence of being a lifelong learner, one who knows how to research, organize information, and continue his or her own learning.

CONCLUSION

We are not interested in gimmicks or bribes that temporarily gain students' attention. Yes, in truth, we have used those tools out of desperation. We want students to engage in learning and benefit from the hard work of their teachers. We want students to develop skills they own and can use in various settings, and not be dependent on their teachers to decide when specific learning tools should be used. And we want students to share responsibility for learning with their teachers and peers. In other words, we want to teach students to drive their learning. We'll explore the metaphor of driving further in the next module. For now, suffice to say that driving requires learning and the transfer of responsibility. Imagine what we can do for our students if we equip them with the skills necessary to increasingly own their learning, understanding that we're all on a path to learning more and better from those around us.

✏️ NOTE TO SELF

John identified the actions and behaviors of highly accomplished, lead teachers. In reality, these teachers did a lot of things differently and used a variety of learning strategies. There is no one right way to teach, but the key is to know whether or not you're having an impact. And when the impact is not acceptable, effective teachers change their approach. The actions that these highly accomplished teachers have in common are shown in the following table. How might you think about these actions in your classroom?

Actions of Highly Accomplished Lead Teachers	What This Could Look Like in My Classroom	Impact on Students
Communicate clear learning intentions		Understand the learning intentions
Have challenging success criteria		Are challenged by success criteria
Teach a range of learning strategies		Develop a range of learning strategies
Know when students are not progressing		Know when they are not progressing
Provide feedback		Seek feedback
Visibly learn themselves		Visibly teach themselves

TEACHER ACTIONS

In each module in this playbook, we provide a list of actions we have observed in classrooms. Sometimes, well-intentioned teachers derail their efforts to create the learning environment that they want. Other times, their actions develop students' skills and knowledge. Consider the following actions that reinforce or derail efforts to ensure that students understand what it means to engage. How can teachers use (or avoid using) these actions to focus on teaching students to drive their learning? We have included blank lines for you to add your ideas.

Teacher Actions That Reinforce Students' Understanding About Engagement	Teacher Actions That Derail Students' Understanding About Engagement
• Teaching students how to engage as explicitly as they teach academic content and language development	• Assuming students know how to monitor their level of engagement
• Recognizing that student acts of disruption, avoidance, or withdrawal are often attempts to hide struggles	• Taking it personally when a student is actively disengaged
• Changing the approach when it's not proving to be effective	• Accepting participation as the end goal
• Providing clear criteria for success, so students can ask for specific feedback	• Expecting students to engage in behaviors that have not been explicitly defined and modeled
• Modeling being a lifelong learner; divulging to students the teacher's own goals in improving their teaching craft	• Continuing with the same approach despite evidence that it is not having the desired impact
_____	_____
_____	_____
_____	_____
_____	_____
_____	_____
_____	_____
_____	_____
_____	_____
_____	_____
_____	_____
_____	_____
_____	_____
_____	_____

RETELLING PYRAMID

Retelling content positively impacts learning as learners summarize information and share it in their own words (Morrow, 1985; Qin et al., 2019). Using a retelling pyramid is one way to encourage and support retellings of informational texts. Create a pyramid of words, using the following prompts, that provides summarizing information. You're more likely to remember this information if you share with a peer.

1. One word that conveys an important topic in this module

2. Two words that convey the value of an engagement continuum

3. Three words for actions you can take based on this module

4. Four words that are key to your understanding

5. Five words that convey a goal you have based on this module

              _____

   _____   _____

 _____   _____   _____

_____ _____ _____ _____

_____ _____ _____ _____ _____

Revisit the Text Impression summary you developed at the beginning of this module, and compare it to your current level of understanding. Where did your learning deepen?

_____

_____

_____

_____

_____

_____

_____

_____

_____

_____

_____

_____

_____

Using the traffic light scale, with red being not confident, yellow being somewhat confident, and green indicating very confident, how confident are you in your ability to

- Discuss the value of viewing engagement as a continuum?

- Describe each of the levels of engagement and identify student actions at each level?

- Identify factors that allow students to drive their learning?

2

LEARNERS KNOW THEIR CURRENT LEVEL OF UNDERSTANDING

LEARNING INTENTION

We are learning how to support students as they define their current level of understanding.

SUCCESS CRITERIA

- I can determine the types of initial assessments that support student and teacher understanding of current learning.

- I can foster academic self-assessment (ASA).

- I can engage in conversations to validate and challenge students' assessment of their own performance.

- I can engage students in estimating task difficulty.

Nancy fondly remembers Sunday drives with her family. They would all pile into the car and head out. The driver (her dad) did not seem to have a specific location in mind, and they visited a variety of places each week, rarely going to the same place twice. But when it was time to return home, the driver would consult a map, and the first thing he did was to identify their current location. Perhaps the driver and navigator (mom) had discussed potential sites to visit in advance, but that was invisible to Nancy. What was clear is that you had to know where you were to be able to get home.

Of course, that's not the only driving that Nancy did with her family. On one Saturday per month, she got to go to work with her dad. On these days it was very clear where they were going, and they would generally follow the same route unless there was a need to get gas, pick up something, or drop a sibling off along the way. Again, Nancy noted that it was important to know where you were starting so that navigation could be successful.

Driving learning is much like driving a car—you need to know where you are if you want to arrive at a desired destination. Even when you are wandering along seemingly for pleasure, when an idea comes to mind, say to visit the swap meet, you have to know where you are if you want to successfully arrive. Although there is much more to academic learning, which we will explore further in this playbook, the basis is knowing your current level of understanding. We chose the word *understanding*, but we could have said performance, learning, competence, or skill. Irrespective of the learning goal, it's important for students to know where they are right now.

> We need to create learning environments that recognize that we are all on a journey and that as long as we are making progress toward the goals, we are learning.

TEXT IMPRESSION

Use the following words (in any order that works for you) to create an impression about what you expect will be covered in this module.

initial assessment • self-assessment • concept map • competency • know/show • rubric • metacognition • task difficulty

_____

_____

_____

_____

_____

_____

_____

_____

_____

_____

_____

_____

_____

Recognizing that students in a given class may vary widely in terms of their current levels of understanding and proficiency, there has been a trend in schools to hide performance levels from students. The logic goes: We don't want to embarrass a student when they realize that some peers may be more advanced in their learning. Of course, we do not want students to be embarrassed by their current performance levels. If they are, it's a sign that the classroom climate needs attention. As we will see in Module 6, for students to drive their learning, they need to recognize mistakes as opportunities to learn. And we need to create learning environments that recognize we are all on a journey, and as long as we are making progress toward the goals, we are learning. Here are a few lessons learned from students regarding their current levels of understanding:

> It's important to set aside time during class to confer with students about their current levels of understanding.

- First grader Kiana explained her writing and compared it with the writing stages used in her classroom. She said, "Some people are right here (pointing to Level 2), and I used to be right here (pointing to Level 3), but now I can put spaces between my words, and I know how to write the words with capital letters. Next, I'm going over to here (pointing to Level 5), and I will make sure that I have periods and that my sight words are right."

- Sixth grader Jordan was working through a math problem and asked a peer, "I'm still trying to remember the right way to round when we have decimals. Can you explain the rule to me again so I can try this one?"

- High school junior Asher asked, "How come no one told me before that I wasn't reading as good as I thought? I always thought that I was at least average for reading. But now I learned I am behind and need to do a lot of work to be ready for college."

Notice that these students make several interesting points. First, as Kiana implies, there is no bad place to be. And knowing where you are helps you set goals for the future. As Jordan notes, knowing what you still need to learn allows you to seek help and feedback. And Asher notes that it's not fair to hide the truth from students. Having information can be empowering and allows students to set goals for themselves. Thankfully, these students attend schools where their teachers understand the value of teaching students to drive their learning.

NOTES

PAUSE AND PONDER

Have you had an honest conversation with a student about their current level of understanding? How does that feel? Have you been taught that we hide this type of information from students and their families?

_____

_____

_____

_____

_____

_____

_____

_____

_____

Before we discuss ways that teachers can successfully ensure that students know where they stand in learning and understanding, it's important to note that we are not suggesting that teachers create a display for the wall that announces all students' performance levels and targets. Although this may be common in sports, as is done with personal bests, it is rare to display academic information for everyone to see. Instead, teachers have several tools that they can use to ensure that students know their current level of understanding. We'll discuss three of these options: initial assessments, self-assessment, and estimating task difficulty. You don't have to use these, but we do suggest that you find a way to ensure that students know their current level of understanding.

It's important to set aside time during class to confer with students about their current levels of understanding. These do not have to be long, drawn-out conversations, but students appreciate the investment of time in them as learners, knowing that you know their current level of understanding and will help them understand what the data means.

INITIAL ASSESSMENTS

Initial assessments can also reduce the number of minutes spent on things students already know.

Assessing what students know in advance of instruction sheds light on the gap between where they are and where you want them to go. Assessment tools can also motivate students when they recognize that there are still things to learn. Interestingly, there has been some pushback on initial assessments, as they may embarrass students or divert valuable instructional minutes away from learning. But without this information, how will students know their starting point? Of course, there are assessment tools that don't yield useful information, but to throw out all initial assessments is unwise.

Parenthetically, initial assessments can also reduce the number of minutes spent teaching things students already know. Nuthall (2007) noted that, on average, about 40% (and maybe more) of instructional minutes are spent on things students already know. Not only is this boring and a waste of time, "teaching" content that some, or all, of the students know does not allow them to drive their learning. In addition, initial assessments allow teachers and students to determine the impact of their efforts. Without information about initial levels of understanding, it's hard to determine if the efforts (instructional events, studying, practice, peer support, or whatever) made a difference. In fact, teachers may take credit for teaching and students may take credit for learning something that was actually acquired long ago.

Imagine that you are teaching argument writing, and you ask your students to write a short essay in which they argue a point and provide evidence. In doing so, you can identify which areas of the standard students already have mastered and where your lessons can contribute to students' progress. You will probably not be the last teacher to focus on argument writing with your students, as it is a skill that takes years to hone. But you can contribute to your students' skill set and ensure that they are on track with the expectations for their grade level. Some students may need help with the type of evidence they provide; others with making a claim. And still others may have difficulty stringing sentences along.

NOTES

 CONNECTIONS

Consider the following questions as you develop an initial assessment to identify what students already know.

Considerations	Your Response
What do I already know about my students from previous units of instruction?	
What type(s) of assessment items will help me identify areas of prior learning: ☐ **Writing sample** ☐ **Oral language or interview** ☐ **Knowledge inventory** ☐ **Other**	How will I collect this information?
How can I ensure that my initial assessments are free from bias?	

Initial assessments do not need to be particularly long or elaborate. Listed below are a few examples teachers have used, but we know that there are many more possibilities:

- Kindergarten teachers collaborated to develop a readiness inventory that included numbers, letters, sight words, colors, et cetera. They decided to administer this individually to get to know each of their students.

- Second-grade teachers provided students with a partially completed concept map illustrating the conceptual relationships between words in the content that was to be taught. The A–Z charts had spaces for students to list words they already knew about the topic they were going to study. In advance of a unit on bats, nearly every student had the terms *flying, wings,* and *vampire* on their charts, and others had terms such as *mammal, fruit,* and *insects.*

- Third-grade teachers used a writing checklist to review students' performance from the previous year. In addition, they collected writing samples each month to monitor progress and make adjustments to the learning intentions for students.

- Middle school math teachers created a tool focused on ratios and rates. They scaled the items along a continuum of complexity. For example, the first item asked the ratio of squares to circles based on an image of three squares and two circles. More complex items focused on equivalent ratios and proportions.

- High school science teachers used a vocabulary assessment to determine students' understanding of key technical terms in advance of the unit on ecology, including *biosphere, biotic, biome, habitat, niche, mutualism, carnivore, herbivore,* and *omnivore.*

Figure 2.1 on the next page provides an assessment tool developed by a first-grade team for initial assessment and monitoring of students' writing. Note that this team is focused on noticing patterns of errors so that they can appropriately group students for instruction. They also use this tool to ensure that students know where they are in the learning journey and to invite students to set writing goals, such as using ending punctuation, spelling their sight words correctly, using capital letters, and so on.

We could go on, as there are many tools that teachers can use to determine what students already know and where they are in their learning journey. Our point is that teachers need to know what their students have already learned and what they still need to learn at the start of the year and at the beginning of each major unit of instruction.

Figure 2.1   Error Analysis for First-Grade Writing

Common Errors	Week 1	Week 2	Week 3	Week 4	Week 5	Week 6
Letter reversals						
Capital letters in the middle of a word						
Misspellings of grade-level sight words						
Misspellings of grade-level spelling patterns (cvc, cvc silent e, digraphs ch, th, sh, wh)						
Sentences do not begin with capital letters						
Sentences do not end with correct punctuation						
Improper use of pronouns						
Beginning a sentence with *And*						
Beginning of the sentence lacks variety						
Sentence doesn't make sense						

✏️ NOTE TO SELF

Take inventory of your assessment tools. Use these questions to guide your process.

Questions	Notes and Reflections
What assessments of prior student learning do I currently have access to?	
How can I gather information to determine what students already know?	
How can I collect information on student strengths to build upon?	
How can I collect information to determine what areas of learning need improvement?	
What strengths do I have in regard to data collection and analysis?	
What opportunities do I have in data collection and analysis?	
What additional information do I need to determine current student performance levels?	

SELF-ASSESSMENT

Academic self-assessment (ASA) is the metacognitive process in which students examine their own work or abilities. This should be considered a core competency for fostering the necessary self-regulation skills that accelerate student learning (Brown & Harris, 2014, p. 27). Andrade (2019) notes, however, that while much has been written about the mechanics of self-assessment, such as the use of rubrics, self-ratings, and estimates of performance, far less has been discussed about the purpose of self-assessment. The true purpose of ASA, she asserts,

> is to generate feedback that promotes learning and improvements in performance. This learning-oriented purpose of self-assessment implies that it should be formative: If there is no opportunity for adjustment and correction, self-assessment is almost pointless. (p. 2)

Self-assessment is at the heart of Visible Learning. Students who can self-assess "exhibit the self-regulatory attributes that seem most desirable for learners (self-monitoring, self-evaluation, self-assessment, self-teaching)" (Hattie, 2012, p. 14).

Many assessment tools are useful in helping students identify their current level of understanding. Of course, these tools can also be used for students to monitor their progress, as we will see in Module 5. For now, we'll focus on the use of self-assessment as a tool to identify current levels of understanding.

PAUSE AND PONDER

Have you ever had the opportunity to self-assess your own learning? How did it feel? What did you do with the results? And how might you use self-assessments for students to infer their current level of understanding?

_____

_____

_____

_____

_____

_____

_____

_____

_____

One example is a know/show chart, which is an open-ended way for students to assess their own understanding. The tool itself is a fairly simple graphic organizer that invites students to identify what they know, based on the expected learning and how they can show what they know. For example, Figure 2.2 was submitted by a student in her U.S. history class. The teacher reviewed the students' "know" column to identify concepts that students reported they understood, which concepts might be confusing, and if there were misconceptions.

Figure 2.2   Know/Show Chart

What I Know	How Can I Show It?
I know what the American Dream is and different perspectives of it.	I can explain my understanding of the American Dream and my perception of it.
I know about the preamble and the purpose of it.	I can delineate in CER form what the preamble portrays and the importance of it in the Constitution.
I learned about the amendment and the freedoms they include, as well as the Bill of Rights.	I can list the 5 freedoms of expression guaranteed in the First Amendment as well as the first 10 amendments (Bill of Rights). I can also list the 6 basic principles of the Constitution and why the Constitution is a living document.
I know about the three branches of the government and how they function.	I can elucidate the three branches of government, their jobs, powers, and who they work for. I can also break down the process of adding an amendment to the Constitution.

Popularized by the Cult of Pedagogy (Gonzalez, 2014), single-point rubrics contain a list of performance or learning expectations. Unlike analytic rubrics, single-point rubrics describe only the criteria for proficiency rather than all the ways in which students could miss the mark or exceed expectations. Originally, these were used by educators to provide students feedback that they could more easily understand, given that there was a lot less language on the tool. But they can be used for students to assess their own understanding at the outset of the lessons.

For example, fourth graders were learning to retell content that they had read, recording their retellings on video for submission to their teacher. Students were provided with the following single-point rubric. Note that students were asked to identify opportunities to grow and where they glow.

	Grows	Success Criteria	Glows
Main Ideas		I tell about the main ideas. I give examples of them.	
Supporting Details		My details are linked to the main ideas.	
Sequence		I retell information in the same order as the author.	
Accuracy		I use accurate facts.	
Inferences		I make connections within the text. I can take what the text says and add my background knowledge to make a theory.	

Madlyn, a student in the class, recorded her retelling of *Henry's Freedom Box* (Levine, 2007). After listening to her retelling, Madlyn completed the self-assessment, noting glows on main ideas and details and accuracy. She noted grow opportunities on the other categories. She wrote herself a note about inferences and said that she didn't have a theory. Her teacher reviewed Madlyn's self-assessment and agreed with her glow areas. The teacher also scheduled a time to talk with Madlyn about inferencing. During their conference, Madlyn said, "I don't have a theory. I don't think that the master was good to Henry like the book says. How can you be good when you can give a person away and make them move where they don't want to live?" Their discussion continued about inferences and how Madlyn knew the text well and was allowed to question the author and make her own decisions.

⊞ CONNECTIONS

Find an analytic rubric, and identify the column for proficiency. If the rubric you have selected has five levels of proficiency, it's probably the column that is a four. Which of the items from this column could be used to create a single-point rubric? How might you need to modify the statements to ensure students can use them to self-assess?

_____

_____

_____

_____

_____

_____

_____

_____

_____

_____

_____

_____

Self-assessments can also be used repeatedly as students acquire additional understanding. For example, the students in Grace Kao's sixth-grade English class assessed their own writing to identify areas of strength and need. Students assessed their writing at the start of the year, and then they continued to use their self-assessment tool to monitor their progress (see Figure 2.3). If properly taught and implemented, the relative accuracy of peer assessments is comparable to that of teacher assessments (Sanchez et al., 2017). And teachers can have powerful conversations with their students in which they validate and challenge students' assessment of their own performance.

Metacognition (thinking about one's thinking) isn't solely about knowing when you know something. It is also the ability to recognize when you don't know something. The ability to think metacognitively helps students make decisions about their own learning. Learners who are metacognitively aware are accurately able to articulate their own strengths and plan for the use of other strategies, including help seeking, that will help them get "unstuck." As John likes to say, "It's knowing what to do when you don't know what to do." Figure 2.4 provides some direction for students who are unsure of what to do.

> Self-assessments can also be used repeatedly as students acquire additional understanding.

Figure 2.3   Comparative Self-Assessment for Informational Writing in Sixth Grade

Title and Date of First Essay				Title and Date of Second Essay			
Organization/Purpose							
Topic is introduced clearly to preview what is to follow				Topic is introduced clearly to preview what is to follow			
4	3	2	1	4	3	2	1
Ideas and concepts are organized using definition, classification, or compare/contrast				Ideas and concepts are organized using definition, classification, or compare/contrast			
4	3	2	1	4	3	2	1
Transitions create cohesion and show relationships among ideas				Transitions create cohesion and show relationships among ideas			
4	3	2	1	4	3	2	1
A concluding statement supports the explanation given				A concluding statement supports the explanation given			
4	3	2	1	4	3	2	1
Task, purpose, and audience are aligned to prompt				Task, purpose, and audience are aligned to prompt			
4	3	2	1	4	3	2	1
Evidence/Elaboration							
Topic is developed with relevant facts, definitions, details, and examples				Topic is developed with relevant facts, definitions, details, and examples			
4	3	2	1	4	3	2	1
Follows a standard format for citations				Follows a standard format for citations			
4	3	2	1	4	3	2	1
Skillfully quotes and paraphrases				Skillfully quotes and paraphrases			
4	3	2	1	4	3	2	1
Uses relevant information from multiple sources				Uses relevant information from multiple sources			
4	3	2	1	4	3	2	1
Effective and appropriate style enhances content				Effective and appropriate style enhances content			
4	3	2	1	4	3	2	1
Conventions							
Demonstrates grade-level grammar, usage, and conventions				Demonstrates grade-level grammar, usage, and conventions			
4	3	2	1	4	3	2	1

Source: Fisher, Frey, Bustamante, and Hattie (2021).

Available for download at **resources.corwin.com/teachingstudentstodrivetheirlearning**

Figure 2.4   Getting Unstuck

I Can't Get Started in My Learning	
What can I do on my own?	☐ I reread the direction to make sure I didn't miss something.
	☐ I reviewed the success criteria.
	☐ I reviewed any examples and/or resources provided for my task.
	☐ I looked online for examples of others' work.
What can I do with a peer?	☐ I asked my peer to clarify the task.
	☐ I asked my peer to walk me through the question and/or problem.
	☐ I asked my peer how they knew how to get started.
	☐ I asked my peer to support me in getting the task started.
What can I do with the teacher?	☐ I clarified what the task is asking for.
	☐ I walked through an example/exemplar with the teacher.
	☐ I asked the teacher to support me in getting the task started.

I Got Started, But I'm Not Sure Where to Go Next in My Learning	
What can I do on my own?	☐ I reviewed the success criteria.
	☐ I reviewed any examples and/or resources provided for my task.
	☐ I tried to determine where I need to go next, based on what I got started.
	☐ I determined what I got right so far and why.
What can I do with a peer?	☐ I clarified what the task was asking for.
	☐ I showed my work to my peer and asked for help in identifying my next step.
	☐ I asked my peer to ask me questions about what I got started on my task.
	☐ I asked my peer what they felt I had gotten right so far and why.
What can I do with my teacher?	☐ I clarified what the task is asking for.
	☐ I asked for support in identifying my next step.
	☐ I asked the teacher to model the portion of the task I misunderstood.

I Finished With My Learning	
What can I do on my own?	☐ I self-assessed my work against the success criteria.
	☐ I reviewed my work against the exemplar, if applicable.
	☐ I identified where I have strengths in my work to get even stronger.
	☐ I identified opportunities in my work to determine what my next learning step is.

(Continued)

(Continued)

I Finished With My Learning	
What can I do with a peer?	☐ I asked my peer if they agree that I met the success criteria.
	☐ I asked my peer to identify strengths in my work.
	☐ I asked my peer to identify an opportunity in my work.
What can I do with my teacher?	☐ I asked my teacher if they agree that I met the success criteria.
	☐ I asked the teacher to identify a strength in my current work.
	☐ I asked the teacher to identify an opportunity in my current work.

Source: Fisher et al. (2018).

ESTIMATING TASK DIFFICULTY

Asking students to estimate the task difficulty can foster their ability to accurately assess their current level of understanding. For example, a teacher may ask students to review an upcoming task and answer four questions about the assignment:

- What will be the easiest part of this assignment?
- What will be the most difficult?
- How much time do I expect it will take me?
- Can I envisage what a successful assignment would look like?

> Learners who are metacognitively aware are accurately able to articulate their own strengths and plan for the use of other strategies, including help seeking, that will help them get "unstuck."

In estimating difficulty, students must consider what they know and can do as well as what they expect will be difficult for them. They may not be totally accurate in their estimation, but the *process* of estimating task difficulty helps students understand where they are in the learning journey.

Most instructional materials (textbooks and other resources) include a list of major outcomes or objectives for each unit or chapter. But how often do we share those with our students? To help students grasp their current level of understanding, teachers can use these lists in advance of instruction by inviting them to rank the objectives according to perceived difficulty. For example, fifth-grade teacher Karin Escartin lists standards from state curriculum units and asks students to rank them in order of perceived difficulty. Before a unit titled "The Legacy for Us Today," Ms. Escartin shared these grade-level expectations and asked each student to rank them:

- I understand that significant historical events in the United States have implications for current decisions and influence the future.
- I can evaluate how a public issue relates to constitutional rights and the common good.
- I understand that civic participation involves being informed about how public issues are related to rights and responsibilities.

- I can research multiple perspectives to take a position on a public or historical issue in a paper or presentation.

- I can evaluate the relevance of facts used in forming a position on an issue or event.

- I can engage others in discussions that attempt to clarify and address multiple viewpoints on public issues based on key ideals.

- I can prepare a list of sources—including the title, author, type of source, date published, and publisher for each source—and arrange the sources alphabetically.

As Ms. Escartin notes,

> I review the "I can" statements with the class and then have them put them in rank order from most difficult to least difficult using the survey tool in our school's learning management system. I get the results, which help me to target instruction and supports and to differentiate a bit more precisely. But it also has a great effect on students, too. They are actively thinking about their current knowledge and skills and making a plan for where they will need to devote more time and effort. I also have them revisit their rankings as we get nearer to the end of the unit, so they can decide how accurate they have been in predicting their current status and what it took to be successful.

Of course, there are other ways for students to estimate task difficulty, such as these:

- Second grader Hamza looked at his spelling list, which focused on *r*-controlled vowels, and noted that he could already spell *stork*, *storm*, *market*, *partner*, and *artist*.

- Seventh grader Ariel completed a checklist about his knowledge and experiences in advance of a unit on the history of the theater, noting for each of the terms one of the following:

  o I have seen a play on TV or at a movie theater.

  o I have seen a live production.

  o I have been in a production.

  o This will be a new experience for me.

- In their high school government class, students brainstormed a list of technical vocabulary and then ranked themselves on their knowledge of each of the terms. As Harper noted, "I knew someone in the class knew the word, but none of us knew them all, so it was easy for me to show which ones I didn't know or only knew a little."

 TEACHER ACTIONS

Consider the following actions that reinforce or derail efforts to ensure that students know their current level of understanding. We have included blank lines for you to add your ideas.

Teacher Actions That Reinforce Students' Recognition of Their Current Level of Understanding	Teacher Actions That Derail Students' Recognition of Their Current Level of Understanding
• Conferencing with students about the data	• Choosing not to share student's data with them
• Devoting time to student self-assessment or initial assessments	• Creating experiences that shame or humiliate students based on their current level of understanding
• Identifying success criteria and inviting students to identify which of these will be difficult for them	• Short-changing the amount of time required for students to self-assess
• Creating a climate of risk taking and understanding that learning occurs across a continuum (and there are no bad places to be)	• Publicly comparing students based on their current levels of understanding
_____	_____
_____	_____
_____	_____
_____	_____
_____	_____
_____	_____
_____	_____
_____	_____
_____	_____
_____	_____
_____	_____
_____	_____
_____	_____

CONCLUSION

It's not enough for teachers to know their students' current performance levels. Students must understand, and use, this information as well. We don't, however, want to minimize the value of teachers knowing their students' current levels of understanding. Using this information allows teachers to plan lessons and move learning forward. Without clear knowledge of students' current knowledge and skill development, teachers run the risk of wasting a lot of time teaching things that students already know and can do. Equipped with good information about students' current performance levels, teachers can establish appropriate learning intentions and success criteria, which are the focus of the next module.

In addition to understanding their current level of understanding, students who drive their learning have to be comfortable sharing their learning progression with others, including their peers and teachers. When their teachers foster habits of seeking out and knowing one's current status and future direction, students can ultimately answer these questions: *Where am I now? Where am I going?* In doing so, students assume increased responsibility for their learning, become their own teachers, and drive their learning, which is the ultimate goal of schooling. Our hopes are not that we create adult-dependent learners, but rather independent learners who continue to seek out information, generate ideas, and influence the world around them.

> Equipped with good information about students' current performance levels, teachers can establish appropriate learning intentions and success criteria.

NOTES

RETELLING PYRAMID

Create a pyramid of words, using the following prompts, that provides summarizing information. You're more likely to remember this information if you share with a peer.

1. One word that conveys an important topic in this module

2. Two words for a type of assessment discussed in this module

3. Three words for actions you can take based on this module

4. Four words that are key to your understanding

5. Five words that convey a goal you have based on this module

_____

_____   _____

_____   _____   _____

_____   _____   _____   _____

_____   _____   _____   _____   _____

Revisit the Text Impression summary you developed at the beginning of this module and compare it to your current level of understanding. Where did your learning deepen?

_____

_____

_____

_____

_____

_____

_____

_____

_____

_____

_____

_____

_____

Using the traffic light scale, with red being not confident, yellow being somewhat confident, and green indicating very confident, how confident are you in your ability to

- Determine the types of initial assessments that support student and teacher understanding of current learning?

- Foster academic self-assessment (ASA)?

- Engage in conversations to validate and challenge students' assessment of their own performance?

- Engage students in estimating task difficulty?

3

LEARNERS UNDERSTAND WHERE THEY'RE GOING

and Have the Confidence to Take on the Challenge

LEARNING INTENTION

We are learning to foster student confidence to take on the challenge of a clearly defined goal.

SUCCESS CRITERIA

- I can explain the relationships between standards, learning intentions, and success criteria.

- I can identify the relevance statements communicated to students across a relevance continuum.

- I can consider success criteria related to standards, engagement, and dispositions.

- I can identify the factors that contribute to motivation in learning and aspiring to be challenged.

There are really two parts to this aspect of teaching students to drive their learning. First, they need to know where they are going. In part, this requires that students understand what they are supposed to be learning. Remember, they will compare this with what they already know and can do. The second part is that students develop the confidence to take on the challenge of learning.

Challenge is an important aspect of learning. As John notes, the "goldilocks" level of challenge, meaning not too hard and not too boring, actually helps students learn more. The effect size of challenging learning tasks is 0.74, above average in its potential to accelerate learning. But students can only accept the challenge of learning if they know what they are supposed to be learning.

> When teachers and students know what needs to be learned and what successful learning looks like, educators can design organized experiences to ensure that students develop increased proficiency.

In this module, we'll focus on the foundation for teacher clarity, which is learning intentions and success criteria. *Teacher clarity*, defined as "a measure of the clarity of communication between teachers and students—in both directions" (Fendick, 1990, p. 10), elegantly captures the reciprocity that is necessary for learning to occur. When teachers and students know what needs to be learned and what successful learning looks like, organized experiences can be designed to ensure that students developed increased proficiency. Of course, establishing the learning intentions and success criteria helps learners in understanding where they are going in their learning. But these instructional moves on their own would be insufficient for learning. Students also need to select tools and learning strategies, monitor their progress, and seek teacher clarity feedback to have the promised impact. Those topics will come in due time. For now, it's important to get the basics right: learning intentions and success criteria.

TEXT IMPRESSION

Use the following words (in any order that works for you) to create an impression about what you predict will be covered in this module.

teacher clarity • relevance • challenge • motivation • goldilocks • self-efficacy • track progress • monitor success

_____

_____

_____

_____

_____

_____

_____

_____

_____

_____

Students thrive when their teachers have clarity about how instruction is organized and delivered. Both teacher and student are engaged in communication about the lesson and the learning that should accompany it. Hattie notes that teacher clarity has a respectable influence on learning, with an effect size of 0.85. The four dimensions of teacher clarity outlined by Fendick (1990) are these:

1. **Clarity of organization** demonstrated through a logical sequencing of tasks that align with learning intentions and success criteria

2. **Clarity of explanation** signified by cohesiveness and accuracy

3. **Clarity of examples and guided practice** that illustrate skills and concepts and move students toward increasing levels of independence

4. **Clarity of assessment of student learning** through frequent checks for understanding and formative evaluation that is responsive to learning needs

NOTES

CONNECTIONS

Review the differences between standards, learning intentions, and success criteria:

Standards	Learning Intentions	Success Criteria
The standards provide us with *concise, written descriptions* of what students are expected to know and be able to do at a specific stage of their education. Standards are written by educators or policy makers for educators.	Learning intentions *adapt the language of the standards into student friendly and manageable statements.* Learning intentions are broken down from the standards into lesson-sized chunks. They are statements of what a student is expected to **learn.** Learning intentions are written by educators for students.	Success criteria *provide a means for students and teachers to measure progress.* They serve to indicate what the intended destination of learning looks like. Success criteria are fundamental in making learning visible to both the teacher and the student. Success criteria are written by educators for students or collaboratively developed with students.

How does this information fit with your understanding? How might you explain the differences to a peer? What other terminology have you heard used for these concepts? (We don't get hung up on the semantics, as there are many terms in education that are used to describe standards, learning intentions, and success criteria.)

_____

_____

_____

_____

_____

_____

_____

_____

_____

_____

LEARNING INTENTIONS

At the heart of what teachers accomplish (or don't) are the goals set for students. There is much talk about having high expectations for students. This goes beyond the state, territory, or provincial standards guiding schools. While standards document the stated learning goals, they are not sufficiently detailed for creating the manageable progressions that lead the learner toward success. These daily steps come in the form of the learning intentions the teacher lays out for students to communicate what they need to learn each day. They ensure that students are able to answer the first clarity question: *What am I learning today?*

There are several reasons why these work so well. First, stated learning intentions have a priming effect on learners. They signal to the student what the purpose is for learning, and they prevent students from falling back to a low rung on the engagement continuum, which is compliance. A second reason why learning intentions are so effective is that they cause students to see the relationship between the tasks they are completing and the purpose for learning. Students need to understand that a particular math activity is for the purpose of building conceptual understanding, or that the assigned reading is to build the background knowledge they'll need for the lab experiment they'll soon be completing.

Consider the following English language arts standard for seventh grade:

> Determine or clarify the meaning of unknown and multiple-meaning words and phrases based on *seventh-grade reading and content*, choosing flexibly from a range of strategies.
>
> a. Use context (e.g., the overall meaning of a sentence or paragraph, a word's position or function in a sentence) as a clue to the meaning of a word or phrase.
>
> b. Use common, grade-appropriate Greek or Latin affixes and roots as clues to the meaning of a word (e.g., belligerent, bellicose, rebel).
>
> c. Consult general and specialized reference materials (e.g., dictionaries, glossaries, thesauruses), both print and digital, to find the pronunciation of a word or determine or clarify its precise meaning or its part of speech.
>
> d. Verify the preliminary determination of the meaning of a word or phrase (e.g., by checking the inferred meaning in context or in a dictionary).

That's way too much to cover in a day, or even in a week or month! Notice that students will have to *determine* or *clarify*, which are skills. They also need to *choose flexibly* and *use context*—again, skills. And they need to understand context clues, affixes, and roots as well as resources, which are concepts.

Learning intentions ensure that students are able to answer the first clarity question: *What am I learning today?*

PAUSE AND PONDER

What might be two learning intentions, something that students could learn in a day, based on this standard?

Sample 1:

_____

_____

_____

_____

_____

_____

_____

_____

Sample 2:

_____

_____

_____

_____

_____

_____

_____

_____

_____

_____

SUCCESS CRITERIA

Success criteria let students in on the secret that has been too often kept from them—what the destination looks like. Imagine getting into an airplane that was being flown by a pilot who didn't know where she was headed. Rather, a control tower would contact her at some unspecified time in the future to let her know she had arrived, or worse, that she missed the mark entirely. That would be a completely irrational way to fly a plane. Yet students often have a similar experience. They're flying their own learning plane but have little sense of where they are headed. Wouldn't the trip be completed more successfully and efficiently if the pilot knew where she was going from the beginning? Now imagine how much more successful and efficient

Success criteria empower learners to assess their own progress.

learning would be if we enlisted students to guide themselves in their learning journeys! Success criteria signal the learner about the destination and provide a map for how they will get there.

Further, success criteria empower learners to assess their own progress and not to be overly dependent on an outside agent (their teacher) to notice when they have arrived. That does not mean that the teacher is unimportant, or that teachers do not need to evaluate students' learning. Like the people in a control tower, the teacher is providing corrective feedback, giving data the pilot can use, and advising her about when and where to proceed. But the important point here is that the pilot and the control tower coordinate their work. One without the other would be unthinkable.

The evidence on the effectiveness of learning intentions and success criteria is impressive. Hattie and Donoghue (2016) examined 31 meta-analyses of more than 3,300 studies related to success criteria and reported an overall effect size of 0.88. Embedded within these studies is evidence of effects on the learner, especially in causing students to plan and predict, set goals, and acquire a stronger sense of how to judge their own progress.

Although there are many ways for teachers to share the criterion for success with students (e.g., Almarode et al., 2021), "I can . . ." statements are a common approach. Of course, teachers can also use checklists, modeling, rubrics, language charts, and a variety of other tools to ensure that students understand what learning looks like. For example, a group of primary grade teachers developed a four-level rubric on partner talk to show what success looked like at each level (see Figure 3.1). Students were asked to use the rubric to decide where they were after talking with a peer.

Figure 3.1   Peer Talk Rubric

Level 1	Level 2
I said something.	I said something.
My partner said something.	My partner said something.
	Then we said MORE!
Level 3	**Level 4**
We talked back and forth.	We talked back and forth.
We asked questions.	We asked questions.
We added onto thinking.	We added and came up with NEW IDEAS!

In another example, a teacher in a chemistry class identified, at the start of the school year, two success criteria for an in-class activity:

- I can describe how subatomic particles affect mass, atomic number, and charge.
- I can calculate the number of neutrons, protons, and electrons in an isotope.

These two success criteria are foundational to understanding and using the periodic table and will serve as the basis for much of the learning students will do in the class. If students do not master these, the teacher will know that she must change the lesson or her strategies. Students can use the success criteria to track their progress, monitor their success against those criteria, seek feedback and assistance when they struggle, and recognize when they have learned something. Our ability to teach students to drive their learning rests on the quality of the success criteria. And success criteria allow students to answer another clarity question: *How will I know I have learned it?*

Importantly, success criteria are not limited to the content students are learning and can include many of the dispositions and social skills that are also the focus of schooling. Using the continuum of engagement that was introduced in Module 1, success criteria might include these:

- I can ask questions when I am confused.
- I can seek help and feedback from my peers.
- I can monitor my nonverbal behaviors and show my partner that I am interested.
- I can take turns when sharing ideas.
- I can use my rubric to ask for specific feedback.
- I can use our checklist to self-assess my learning.
- I can feel like what we are learning is important.
- I can explain why today's learning is important.
- I can use "think time" to formulate my thoughts, so I can participate in the discussion.
- I can think about what my classmates are saying, so I can respond to their ideas.

Said more plainly, when there is something we want students to learn, it's useful if they know what successful learning looks like. That way they can set a goal and monitor their own progress—again, the sign that students are driving their learning.

Figure 3.2 contains a list of learning intentions and success criteria for one school on one day. These are not perfect, but rather actual attempts by teachers to ensure that students know what they are learning and what successful learning looks like.

Figure 3.2   Learning Intentions and Success Criteria: Classroom Example

Grade Level	Example 1: ELA		Example 2: Math		Example 3: Other Content Areas	
PreK	LI:	We are learning about the parts of a book.	LI:	We are learning about different ways to show/represent numbers.	LI:	We are learning to create and share art with others.
	SC:	I can tell where the cover is. I can show pages in the book.	SC:	I can use different objects to count. I can show/represent different numbers with objects.	SC:	I can explain the parts of my drawing to my partner.

Grade Level	Example 1: ELA		Example 2: Math		Example 3: Other Content Areas	
TK/K	LI:	We are learning about rhyming words in poetry.	LI:	We are learning that some numbers are bigger than other numbers.	LI:	We are learning how to throw using an underhand technique.
	SC:	I can name two words that rhyme. I can add a third word with the same rhyme.	SC:	I can compare two numbers and tell you which one is bigger. I can support my telling with objects.	SC:	I can use an underhand-throwing motion to hit a target.
1st	LI:	We are learning how signal words tell the structure of a text.	LI:	We are learning about different approaches to solving addition problems.	LI:	We are learning about cardinal directions.
	SC:	I can retell the text to my partner and use *first, then, next,* and *last* in my retelling.	SC:	I can explain my solution to a partner using a tens frame.	SC:	I can draw a map using map symbols. I can show the cardinal directions on my map.
2nd	LI:	We are learning to ask questions of the author while we read.	LI:	We are learning how to use mental math to count.	LI:	We are learning about water in solid, liquid, and gaseous states.
	SC:	I can record my questions about the text in the margin.	SC:	I can count forward by fives.	SC:	I can explain how to change water into different states of matter.
3rd	LI:	We are learning different ways that authors express opinions.	LI:	We are learning about different ways to display data.	LI:	We are learning about tempo and dynamics in music.
	SC:	I can explain the author's opinion using the author's word choices.	SC:	I can plan, collect, organize, and display my data with a bar graph. I can explain what the bar graph tells me about my data.	SC:	I can describe how the tempo can change the mood or emotion of a piece of music.
4th	LI:	We are learning about sentence fluency in writing.	LI:	We are learning about the differences between prime and composite numbers.	LI:	We are learning about the works of local artists.
	SC:	I can use the rubric to give my partner specific feedback about the types of sentences they use.	SC:	I can provide three examples of prime numbers. I can provide three examples of composite numbers.	SC:	I can explain to my group members about a career in art-making.
5th	LI:	We are learning how an author's choice of word impacts the tone.	LI:	We are learning the placement of decimals and the impact on a number's size.	LI:	We are learning about latitude and longitude.
	SC:	I can select a word from the text and explain to my partner why the author may have chosen it.	SC:	I can explain what happens to a number when the decimal is moved right or left.	SC:	I can find places on a map by using coordinates.
6th	LI:	We are learning how authors introduce key ideas in a text.	LI:	We are learning when to use exponents in the order of operations.	LI:	We are learning about the differences between muscular strength and muscular endurance.
	SC:	I can provide details such as examples and anecdotes that show how ideas are elaborated.	SC:	I can explain how to use the order of operations to evaluate numeric expressions.	SC:	I can discuss examples of muscular strength and muscular endurance with my group.

PAUSE AND PONDER

Review the work of these teachers and consider the following:

What are the trends I am noticing?

_____

_____

_____

_____

_____

What are the characteristics of the learning intentions at this school?

_____

_____

_____

_____

_____

_____

What are the characteristics of the success criteria?

_____

_____

_____

_____

_____

_____

What might I add to these for my students?

_____

_____

_____

_____

_____

_____

RELEVANCE

We can't leave the subject of learning intentions and success criteria before addressing the issue of relevance in learning. Learning intentions and success criteria address the acquisition and consolidation of skills and concepts; relevance addresses motivation to learn. All learners need to have some insight into why they are learning something. Some learning purposes come with relevance baked into them, such as successfully completing a driver's education course to gain a permit or license.

But the relevance of much of the school-based knowledge we teach is not so readily apparent to the learner. It can be a struggle to frame the relevance of content if one possesses a belief that everything needs to lead to a distant and aspirational ending, such as focusing on graduating from college when you're still in fourth grade. Quite frankly, a lot of what we teach doesn't fit into the driver's license kind of scenario, and when the goal is too far in the distance, it's not very motivating. Relevance needs to be closer to home. Why are syllables important? *Because they help us read big words.* Why do we need to know the difference between a simile and a metaphor? *So we can use these techniques in our own writing to express ideas without being too obvious.* Why are we learning to balance equations in chemistry? *Because no substance on Earth can exist if it violates the law of conservation of matter. And because balancing equations allows us to understand how food becomes fuel for our bodies, why soap removes grime, and many other things, including some things you might want to invent on your own.*

> Relevance allows students to answer the final clarity question: *Why am I learning this?*

Taking the time to address relevance not only fosters motivation but also deepens learning, as students begin to connect to larger concepts. In other words, an understanding of the relevance of one's learning moves students forward from declarative (factual) knowledge through to procedural and conditional knowledge—from *what* to *how* to *when*. Relevance allows students to answer the final clarity question: *Why am I learning this?*

For many students, the development of relevance follows success in learning. As it is when they play video games, learning can be self-reinforcing, and when they are learning skills and understanding, students can begin to see the relevance of learning the skills and gaining the knowledge that is fundamental to other and future tasks.

Priniski et al. (2018) define relevance across a continuum from least to most relevant:

- *Personal association* is through a connection to an object or memory, such as enjoying reading about motorcycles because the student is learning to ride one. When students make connections with something outside the classroom, they are much more likely to want to learn more.

- *Personal usefulness* is based on students' beliefs that a task or text will help them reach a personal goal. For example, a child reads articles about soccer, because improving passing skills is valued. Or a student perseveres through a mathematics course because she believes that the knowledge will help her gain admission to a specific college, thus allowing her to study engineering.

- *Personal identification* is the most motivating type of relevance and stems from a deep understanding that the task or text aligns with one's identity. When students get to learn about themselves, their problem solving, and their ability to impact others, relevance is increased. For example, a student who wants to be an artist finds relevance in geometry when perspective is discussed.

When the students in Brad Maddox's fifth-grade class learned about the 1790 decision to move the capital of the United States from Philadelphia and build a permanent capital city in the area we know as the District of Columbia, the teacher said,

> Some people know the history, but a lot of people don't. The politicians of the time wanted to appease Southern states that supported slavery. We've learned about other times when appeasement was used to calm down a group. They didn't want a Northern capital. I think that people who understand why the capital was moved understand political motivation, which can help them out when they want to negotiate. And I think it would be great to talk with your families about the reason that the capital moved. Let's see how many people we can educate!

Consider the following example. Highlight the ways in which the teacher communicates the learning intentions, success criteria, and relevance.

Motivation and interest further expand students' ability to attend to their learning.

Gretchen Harrison has been teaching a unit on the nervous system in her biology class. Today's lesson is on language centers in the brain's cerebral cortex. She gestures to a diagram of the brain in the students' materials: "Today we are learning to understand the functions of Wernicke's area and Broca's area on speech and language, and relate them to specific aphasias."

Ms. Harrison adds, "Based on your understanding of the anatomical features of these two areas, you will explain the physiological results when either is damaged."

She continues, "This is something that at first is going to seem a bit challenging. But I've also witnessed your growing expertise about the nervous system. You've got the tools to accomplish this. I hope we can apply this knowledge to the videos we saw and learn to explain what happened to the people in the videos. And, this knowledge will help us in our quest to understand how our brains work."

The teacher then asked her students to take a few minutes to answer the first two of three metacognitive questions they use when embarking on new content learning. These will be the basis for an exit slip they will submit at the end of class (see Figure 3.3):

1. *What?*

2. *So what?*

3. *What's next?*

Figure 3.3   Reflective Questions

1. **What?** Take a few moments to write down what you already know about this topic. Based on your prior knowledge, what are your predictions? Next, write one or two statements or questions you have about today's topic. What don't you know but hope to learn?

2. **So what?** Relevance is important in learning. Based on what you know and what you hope to learn, in what ways might this affect other body systems?

3. **What's next?** Reflect on today's learning and its implications for future learning. What do you anticipate you will learn about soon? Your ability to predict future concepts based on present knowledge is a good indicator of your learning.

Near the end of the lesson, Ms. Harrison asked students to write their explanation and rationale for Broca's aphasia and Wernicke's aphasia, followed by their third question: *What's next?* The purpose of this question is for students to anticipate what information they will need to deepen their knowledge. Sometimes it is crafted in the form of a statement, but more often it is posed as a question. Lucas wrote the following: "Broca's aphasia makes it hard for the patient to produce sentences more than a few words long. But what gets damaged if they aren't producing any speech at all? It can't be the same area of the brain. I think this is what we'll learn next."

PAUSE AND PONDER

How could you use the three reflective questions—*What? So what? What's next?*—to help students drive their learning?

_____

_____

_____

_____

_____

_____

_____

_____

_____

_____

MOTIVATION IN LEARNING

Motivation and interest further expand students' ability to attend to their learning. Emotion plays an important role in motivation, so first and foremost is considering and developing a positive learning climate. Motivation increases when students see their classroom as a place where mistakes are viewed as opportunities to learn, and learning is seen as a cause for celebration. Another important factor is creating conditions that allow students to become more autonomous in their own learning. And as students are successful in their learning, their motivation can increase. Students gain much motivation from learning (and motivation does not always precede learning). Choice contributes to autonomy and creates positive emotions that fuel learning. However, choice is not the only path for fostering motivation. Challenge is another element that can be utilized to capitalize on motivation. One way to accomplish this is by linking success criteria to various ways to demonstrate mastery of a topic.

Choice is one element that contributes to autonomy and creates positive emotions that fuel learning. Challenge is another element.

Fifth-grade science teacher Aisha Taylor-Brown provides a range of ways her students can show their learning about electrical circuits, including building a simple circuit, drawing a diagram of one, or recording a video in which they explain the process. She asks them to choose a functional use for the circuit, such as powering a digital clock or light bulb. "This is foundational knowledge. I want them to be able to explain the flow of electrons. But it's also a stepping stone to even more choice. The next unit is robotics, and they'll need to use principles of circuitry to make their robots work."

Ms. Taylor-Brown is leveraging another element of motivation, which is interest in the topic. To be sure, some instructional units lend themselves to higher levels of student interest, like robotics in the elementary classroom. But other techniques are likely to tap into student interest, such as examining age-appropriate controversial topics.

Seventh-grade English teacher Kendra Washington used bullying as a theme and allowed students to choose from a curated list of readings, including *Smile* (Telgemeier, 2010), *Wonder* (Palacio, 2012), and *Backlash* (Littman, 2016). "The topic resonates with middle schoolers, and giving them a choice of reading selection is motivating, too," she explained. Ms. Washington begins each semester with an online ballot for her students to vote on unit topics. "I've got more units than I have time to teach, so letting them choose the topics actually helps me a lot." In addition, she requires each of her students to propose and complete an investigation of a research topic every semester. "They propose, and I listen. I've had students choose everything from Laura wanting to learn about self-driving cars to Justin who wanted to develop tips for starting a modeling career. You can't fully anticipate what students' individual interests will be. But if we never ask, how will they be cognizant of their interests and the paths to get there?"

A growth mindset is critical for facing challenges without giving in to defeat.

NOTES

✏️ NOTE TO SELF

Use the following tools to identify practices that are useful in ensuring teacher clarity in terms of learning intentions, success criteria, and relevance. Remember, for students to drive their learning, they should be able to answer the three following clarity questions:

- What am I learning today?
- How will I know that I learned it?
- Why am I learning this?

Learning Intentions

Teacher Practices Learning Intentions	Beginning B	Progressing P	Consistent C	Next Steps
Learning intentions are visible and usable for students.				
Learning intentions are discussed at the beginning, middle, and end of the lesson.				
Students are given time to reflect on, ask questions about, and discuss the learning intentions.				
Connections are made to the learning intentions while students are engaged in the learning.				
Students are asked to monitor their progress using the learning intentions.				
Learning intentions are directly connected to the standard(s).				

Source: Lassiter et al. (2022).

(Continued)

Success Criteria

Teacher Practices Success Criteria	Beginning B	Progressing P	Consistent C	Next Steps
Success criteria are visible and usable for students.				
Success criteria are shared and clarified with students before, during, and after learning.				
Success criteria communicate: *I will know I have learned it when I can . . .* with specific parts or steps needed for success.				
Success criteria include worked examples, exemplars, or models for clarity.				
Students are asked to use the success criteria to self-assess learning progress.				
Students are asked to provide feedback to peers using success criteria.				
Success criteria are used to provide feedback to students.				
Each criterion for success moves the students incrementally closer to the learning intention.				

Source: Lassiter et al. (2022).

Relevance

Teacher Practices Relevance	Beginning B	Progressing P	Consistent C	Next Steps
There is a consideration of the relevance connection for the lesson prior to instruction.				
Relevance statements are closely connected to students and not to a distant goal.				
Providing the relevance statement supports students moving from declarative to procedural and conditional knowledge.				
Relevance statements allow students to make a personal association (a connection to an object or memory).				
Relevance statements promote the belief that a task or text will help students reach a personal goal.				
Relevance is provided so students recognize that the task or text is aligned with their identity and their ability to impact others.				

ASPIRING TO CHALLENGE

Motivation is also sparked by the desire to achieve mastery of a challenging skill or concept. Watch an aspiring athlete practice for hours on layups in basketball or juggling and dribbling techniques in soccer, and you get the idea. In fact, learning can't occur in the absence of challenge—it's stagnation, not progression. Students who drive their learning understand that challenge is necessary on the road to mastery and are resilient in the face of temporary setbacks. A growth mindset is critical for facing challenges without giving in to defeat. But Dweck (2016) warns against the "false growth mindset" that communicates a misunderstanding about its variable nature. "No one has a growth mindset in everything all the time," says Dweck. "Everyone is a mixture of fixed and growth mindsets" (Gross-Loh, 2016).

Most important of all, a growth mindset isn't a state of being—it is a coping skill one chooses (or chooses not) to draw on in the face of challenge. Note this is a key statement. Growth mindsets are not permanent attributes of a student, but this way of thinking can be critical in times of challenge, anxiety, error, and not knowing. And a growth mindset isn't necessary when engaged in an easy task, because there is no need to cope with anything. A growth mindset is fostered in relation to challenge. Students who rarely confront a difficult task are robbed of the opportunity to cultivate a growth mindset. Instead, they are failure deficient. One's mindset is influenced by one's previous experience with the skill or concept. Students who don't know much about a topic of study *and* are aware that they don't know enough yet have an opportunity to cultivate that growth mindset as a means to persevere in the face of an obstacle. But praising their effort while ignoring the failed attempt doesn't help students move toward mastery or to develop a growth mindset. Students need to be able to examine the strategies they used and formulate new plans to try out in the next attempt. One element necessary for doing so is to recognize when they don't know something.

The confidence to take on a challenging learning task involves self-efficacy. Bandura (1997) introduced self-efficacy as a driving force in the learning process, noting that "self-belief does not necessarily ensure success, but self-disbelief assuredly spawns failure" (p. 77). Learners' self-efficacy contributes to their willingness to engage in academic risk taking, a necessary component in the learning equation. As with other constructs internal to the learner, self-efficacy is discipline specific. All of us have experienced rising and diminishing levels of self-efficacy as we traveled from mathematics class to English, from art class to physical education.

Academic self-efficacy is an important factor in self-regulation. Self-regulation involves a collection of behaviors and dispositions, including the ability to self-observe, self-judge, and self-react (Bong, 2013). The ability to self-regulate is mediated by a learner's developmental level and experiences. Students need to be consistently drenched in opportunities to notice their thinking and feelings, make judgments about their status, and act upon their conclusions in ways that are growth producing. Ms. Harrison's *what*, *so what*, and *what's next* questions are designed to prompt self-observation. In addition to maintaining focus, students with strong self-regulatory behaviors choose more challenging tasks, are better at selecting strategies, put forth more effort, and display lower levels of anxiety. Bandura and others (e.g., Caprara et al., 2008) noted that in an increasingly technology-driven world, one in which information is readily available in a few keystrokes, self-efficacy is more critical than ever, because it contributes to flexibility of thought in swiftly changing environments.

> The confidence to take on a challenging learning task involves self-efficacy.

 TEACHER ACTIONS

Consider the following actions that reinforce or derail efforts to ensure that students know where they are going in their learning journey. We have included blank lines for you to add your ideas.

Teacher Actions That Reinforce Students' Knowledge About Where They Are Going and Their Acceptance of the Challenge of Learning	Teacher Actions That Derail Students' Knowledge About Where They Are Going and Their Acceptance of the Challenge of Learning
• Planning out instruction including accurate explanations, examples, and guided practice	• Asking students to set goals without the teacher having a clear understanding of the goal
• Allocating time during instruction for students to understand the path of learning and to self-assess their current progression	• Expecting students to monitor their progress without providing a model for how to self-assess
• Providing choice in how students demonstrate mastery of the success criteria	• Expecting students to monitor progress and set goals without providing time and opportunities to monitor success against the success criteria
• Using student interests to develop learning experiences that resonate with them	• Not recognizing that each year the students have different interests and unique identities
• Promoting academic self-efficacy by immersing students in opportunities to notice their thinking and feelings	
_____	_____
_____	_____
_____	_____
_____	_____
_____	_____
_____	_____
_____	_____
_____	_____
_____	_____
_____	_____
_____	_____
_____	_____
_____	_____

CONCLUSION

Students who drive their learning possess a level of attention and motivation that supports their learning. That attention focuses on a student's current performance level, the expected performance as expressed in a learning intention, and the success criteria that will be used to determine whether or not sufficient learning has occurred. Teachers and students both have roles to play in helping students know where they are going in their learning journey. Of course, students don't all arrive in our classrooms fully actualized. Rather, their teachers build the cognitive and metacognitive habits that make it possible for them to make learning visible to themselves. No child is "unmotivated," but some may have not yet encountered the right formula for unlocking their motivation. In other words, they haven't met you.

Students who drive their learning possess a level of attention and motivation that supports their learning.

NOTES

RETELLING PYRAMID

Create a pyramid of words, using the following prompts, that provides summarizing information. You're more likely to remember this information if you share with a peer.

1. One word that conveys an important topic in this module

2. Two words for ideas you want to explore further

3. Three words for actions you can take based on this module

4. Four words that are key to your understanding

5. Five words that convey a goal you have based on this module

_____

_____   _____

_____   _____   _____

_____   _____   _____   _____

_____   _____   _____   _____   _____

Revisit the Text Impression summary you developed at the beginning of this module, and compare it to your current level of understanding. Where did your learning deepen?

_____

_____

_____

_____

_____

_____

_____

_____

_____

_____

_____

_____

Using the traffic light scale, with red being not confident, yellow being somewhat confident, and green indicating very confident, how confident are you in your ability to

- Explain the relationship between standards, learning intentions, and success criteria?

- Identify the relevance statements communicated to students across a relevance continuum?

- Consider success criteria related to standards, engagement, and dispositions?

- Identify the factors that contribute to motivation in learning and aspiring to be challenged?

4

LEARNERS SELECT TOOLS TO GUIDE THEIR LEARNING

LEARNING INTENTION

We are learning to teach students to select tools that guide their learning.

SUCCESS CRITERIA

- I can explore ideas for providing opportunities for students to practice selecting and using tools and strategies.

- I can describe the principles of deliberate practice.

- I can examine ideas for targeted, distributed, and self-directed practice.

- I can identify examples of cognitive, metacognitive, and affective study skills.

Decisions are essential in the life of learners who know how to drive their learning. Students need opportunities to consider which tools and strategies they will use and for what purposes. Of course, learning tools do not always work in each situation, and students will likely make mistakes and choose the wrong tools sometimes. That's also a good learning opportunity. When students learn, for example, that rereading did not help them this time and they figure out why, they become increasingly strategic about using learning tools. That's not to say that rereading is a bad habit; it can be highly effective in the right context. But sometimes we need to do other things to make sense of the text. We hope that students learn to never hold a learning strategy in higher esteem than their own learning. They need to learn to change the approach if it is not working for them.

It is analogous to the range most of us have experienced with cooking. Some would-be chefs don't progress beyond close adherence to a recipe, never straying far from the steps listed. But others, having mastered the basics, get more creative. Decisions are made based on personal preferences, time restrictions, and availability of ingredients. These cooks can think more strategically, weighing the tools they have at their disposal with the needs of those who will be eating. Students who drive their learning are like those talented cooks in our own families. They can pair tools and strategies with intentions and desired outcomes.

It's difficult to make decisions and solve problems when you don't know where you are or where you're heading. The cook who knows what dish to prepare is much more likely to succeed. In classrooms, learning intentions and success criteria help tremendously when it comes to setting these conditions. But students also need to be able to exert choice and make decisions about their own advancement. Students who drive their learning allow teachers to function more often as "activators and evaluators of learning" (Hattie, 2012, p. 186). This is different from being an evaluator of *learners*, which is about sorting them into categories.

> Students need opportunities to consider which tools and strategies they will use and for what purposes.

TEXT IMPRESSION

Use the following words (in any order that works for you) to create an impression about what you think will be covered in this module.

student decisions • deliberate practice • study skills • memorizing • expertise • selecting tools

_____
_____
_____
_____
_____
_____
_____
_____

THE VALUE OF COGNITIVE TOOLS

To be sure, the tools students need to solve problems and forward their own learning must be taught and regularly used. Strategic applications of tools are mental and intellectual skills, not behavioral ones. Students are going to have a far more difficult time establishing learning habits if they are rarely given the opportunity to use the tools. Unfortunately, we often see lots of energy being expended on teaching initial strategies, with little opportunity to use those strategies under anything other than highly engineered circumstances. Underlining the main idea on a worksheet of paragraphs doesn't enable the student to determine the importance of that idea. Finding the main idea shouldn't be an academic exercise. It should be a strategic tool readers use when they are trying to gain an understanding of something they are reading. Students need to use these and other strategies with purpose, in the context of learning.

Students who drive their learning are actively engaged and can marshal skills and dispositions in order to advance their learning. John speaks often of the need to bring together the skill, the will, and the thrill of learning in our classrooms. Skill is about a learner's knowledge, while will is the learner's disposition. Claxton and Lucas (2016) memorably state that "a skill is something you can do; a disposition is something you are on the look-out for opportunities to do" (p. 7). Bring skill and will together, and add motivation to learn something interesting, and now you have the third ingredient: thrill. School, and learning, should be a thrill. It should be intrinsically motivating to learn and be able to apply what you have learned to new situations.

We could explore several different learning tools, but this playbook is not about specific instructional approaches. Yes, there are illustrative examples of instruction throughout, but it's not about instructional strategies per se. Instead, it is about building habits that allow students to drive their learning. As an example of students learning to select tools, we'll focus on graphic organizers. We discussed motivation and relevance in the last module. This module adds the tools that students need to be able to take action based on their learning goals.

> Students who drive their learning are actively engaged and can marshal skills and dispositions in order to advance their learning.

NOTES

CONNECTIONS

Let's explore skill, will, and thrill a bit further. As Hattie and Donoghue (2016) note, "Developing outcomes in achievement (skill) is as valuable as enhancing the dispositions towards learning (will) and as valuable as inviting students to reinvest more into their mastery of learning (thrill or motivations)." In Figure 4.1, we provide a definition of each, and we encourage you to identify tasks that students could do in your classroom that meet each of the three conditions.

Figure 4.1   The Skill, Will, and Thrill of Learning

Aspect of Learning	Definition	Sample Tasks
Skill	The learned knowledge, concepts, or strategies	
Will	A student's various dispositions toward learning	
Thrill	The motivations held by the student	

ORGANIZING VISUALLY

Visually organized information can help students see connections among the ideas and information they are learning. The key to using graphic organizers is to ensure that students are not simply copying from their teacher. Instead, students need to be given information and then encouraged to select a graphic organizer that will allow them to represent the information. For example, the students in Marco Jimenez's fourth-grade class studied the similarities and differences between the state and federal governments. The students had read from their textbook, watched a video, engaged in a class discussion, and heard their teacher talk about this. They had a lot of information, but Mr. Jimenez knew that they wouldn't remember it, much less be able to use it, if they didn't do something with it.

He asked his students to think about all the graphic organizers they had used and to identify one that they believed would work to capture similarities and differences. Carlos chose a compare-and-contrast diagram, whereas Natalie selected an attribute tool that allowed her to name each factor and then note how it was used in the state and federal governments. In all, the students selected six different tools in Mr. Jimenez's class. Again, a student may have selected a tool that did not work for this task, and that would also be important learning for the student. As noted in the example of graphic organizers, the key is to introduce students to a range of tools, provide them opportunities to practice, and then structure learning tasks so that they make choices about which tools to use.

If you were going to organize the information in this module, which graphic organizers would work for you? Consider the possibilities below and how you might use them.

> Visually organized information can help students see connections between the ideas and information they are learning.

COMMON GRAPHIC ORGANIZERS

Type	Description	Example
Venn	Overlapping circles that illustrate similarities and differences between two concepts	
Web	Central word or phrase linked to supporting labels, concepts, and ideas	
Sequence/ process	Shows a series of steps or a timeline	

(Continued)

(Continued)

Type	Description	Example
Story map	Used to show different elements such as characters, plots, themes, etc.	
Chart/matrix	Rows and columns in a table format that shows relationships vertically and horizontally	
T-chart	Two-column table for grouping ideas into categories	
KWL	Three-column chart for recording what is *known* about a topic, what students *want* to learn, and later, what they have *learned* about the topic	
Frayer	Four-celled table for recording information about a term or concept; the information recorded inside the cells could be examples and nonexamples, definitions, synonyms and antonyms, the term used in context, an illustration or drawing, and more	
Problem-solution map	Identifies a problem and possible solutions, often with pros and cons for each solution	

PAUSE AND PONDER

Which of the graphic organizers in the preceding figure would meet your purpose of visually organizing information from this module?

_____

_____

_____

_____

_____

_____

_____

_____

Which do you think would be a bad choice and why?

_____

_____

_____

_____

_____

_____

_____

_____

_____

_____

THE VALUE OF DELIBERATE PRACTICE

"You can't get good at something you don't do." Or as the golfer Gary Player once remarked, "The more I practice, the luckier I get." Observing others doing something is important for building a model of what a skill or behavior looks like, but without intentional practice, you're not going to build your own skills. (Think of all the cooking/dancing/sports competitions you've watched.) Likewise, students need to practice academic skills to gain fluency and proficiency. Most teachers create opportunities for guided practice as part of their teaching. It is not simply more of the same, more effort, or more grit. Teaching students to drive their learning means going a step further. Teachers need to get students to engage in intentional practice in order for them to acquire and consolidate knowledge. This is what is meant by deliberate practice.

Practice is fundamental to learning, especially when acquiring and consolidating cognitive and motor skills. This means that learners are engaged in deliberate practice, which is not simply rote rehearsal, but rather is difficult and strains the learner. In other words, it is not just *work*, but *work that is hard to do* (Ericsson et al., 1993). Deliberate practice

> Practice is fundamental to learning, especially when acquiring and consolidating cognitive and motor skills.

involves seeking and receiving feedback, and moving beyond what you can do now to tackle more challenging tasks to build on what you know and can do. A basketball player doesn't gain expertise simply by throwing countless free throws from the line in a quiet gym. Players change up the demands by practicing from different locations on the court and testing themselves as they push through a variety of distractions. In other words, players who want to improve make sure the work they do is hard. We are reminded of a quote attributed to martial arts icon Bruce Lee: "I fear not the man who has practiced 10,000 kicks once, but I fear the man who has practiced one kick 10,000 times."

But practice is used for other purposes besides building expertise. Some practice is used to build automaticity such that something becomes increasingly fluent and requires decreasing attention (LaBerge & Samuels, 1974). Automaticity comes from rehearsal and repetition. Learning multiplication facts, sight words, the periodic table of elements, and significant dates and events in a nation's history are all examples of discrete skills and concepts that pave the way for deeper learning. Several rehearsal techniques are excellent for building automaticity, such as flashcards, mnemonics, mapping, and summarizing. These and other study skills have a strong effect size ($d = 0.53$; Hattie, 2023). In fact, we think so highly of study skills instruction that we will devote a later portion of this module to the topic.

But in terms of student factors, the fundamental question for them is being able to say why they are practicing to select the right approach. The third-grade learners in John Kovena's class are challenged to answer this question first before selecting their activity for practicing language. Mr. Kovena explains, "The children at this school are learning to speak and read in Spanish as well as in English. Our language is our culture. We want our young people to be able to speak with their elders and participate in traditions." Mr. Kovena devotes time daily to developing his students' Spanish language skills, including time for practice. Before moving to collaborative and independent practice activities, they must consider their goals. "Are you working on memorizing or on expertise?" he asks, reminding them "you need both. You just need to know why you're doing what you're doing."

The teacher has several possible activities for them to choose from, labeled as either *Desarrollando mi memoria* (Build My Memory) or *Desarrollando mi habilidades* (Build My Expertise). Peter decides that he wants to focus on memorizing and chooses a Spanish vocabulary flashcard game to play with another classmate. Freddy has selected expertise building on this day and settles in to listen to a recording in the Spanish language of a fable told by a volunteer. Another classmate has also selected expertise and has chosen to write a short message in Spanish in a greeting card to her grandmother, using language frames the teacher has prepared. Mr. Kovena speaks briefly with each child, asking about their goals. Peter wants to beat his previous time naming all the vocabulary words in his deck, while Freddy will retell the folktale in Spanish to his teacher. Alice, the student writing to her grandmother, will ask Mr. Kovena to preview her card for errors before sealing it in the envelope. "I wouldn't say there's anything unusual about what [the students] are doing," said the teacher. "I want them to know why and to have choice. Practice works much better when you know what you want out of it."

You can make the most of practice by ensuring that it meets three conditions:

- Targeted
- Distributed
- Self-directed

Targeted practice is useful when developing memorization through rehearsal. Repeated reading, practicing sight words with flashcards, and memorizing multiplication tables are examples of a targeted practice. Students at Health Sciences High compete at the state and national levels in events such as medical spelling, emergency responding, public health information campaigns, and medical photography. One event is a prepared team presentation for public health that must be timed and delivered live to sync with the wordless background video the students develop. The topic changes each year. One year the topic was "Sitting is the New Smoking," and a team of six high school students developed the video and scripted their lines for the five-minute speech. They engaged in weeks of targeted practice as they honed their speaking skills and timed each line. Working first with full scripts, then note cards, and finally without any support, they timed each line so that speakers could adjust the speech rate to pace and coordinate their delivery with the silent video in the background. Perhaps most interesting was the way they rehearsed, chunking each portion into 30-second passages. Only when they felt they had reached mastery of the first segment would they then move on to the second. Gradually, they coupled longer passage strings, until they had memorized the entire presentation. Apparently, it worked, as the team took second in the state and competed in the international competition.

> Goals that have been determined by the student fuel learning in ways that those set by others cannot.

Distributed practice occurs at regular intervals over days and weeks, facilitating acquisition of new knowledge. Most of us have learned from our own failures that cramming for a test the night before the exam rarely delivers satisfactory results. Without regular practice, skills atrophy. Simply said, distributed practice is more effective than mass practice, with an effect size of 0.71. Unfortunately, too many students naïvely believe that an intensive cram session of several hours is just as useful as short daily sessions leading up to an event. Mr. Kovena's decision to set aside time each day for students to practice their Spanish language skills is an example of distributed practice. Eighth-grade student Victor explained it this way to his class in a presentation about learning habits:

> It's like learning to play soccer. I'm working on my dribbling skills right now. Coach sets up cones for us to perform drills. I'd be off the team if I only practiced dribbling for a few hours before the match and didn't touch a soccer ball any other time. Same thing with studying for computer programming tests. If I try to memorize it all the night before, it's a fail.

A third condition of practice is that whenever possible it should be *self-directed*. Goals that have been determined by the student fuel learning in ways that those set by others cannot. A middle school team of teachers introduced Mastery Monday as a way to create opportunities for students to engage in self-directed practice. Students review the results of the previous week's work, including feedback on assignments, and choose an assignment (or portion) they would like to revisit. During a 15-minute segment of the class, they revise responses and resubmit their work. Math teacher Beth Russell said it works especially well in her content area. "Some of the learning they experience by the end of the week is more advanced. Giving them a chance to go back and make corrections to problems from earlier in the week reinforces the learning." Student Ricardo, who had been listening to the conversation, added "I like it when I see the number correct change on the [digital] assignment," he said. "We don't get a grade on these, 'cause our course grades are competency based. We only get grades on the unit tests. But I like seeing the green bar for the number correct get higher."

✏️ NOTE TO SELF

In your content area, what type of practice builds expertise? What type develops automaticity? What are some ways you could incorporate practice that is targeted, distributed, and self-directed?

Ideas for Targeted Practice	Ideas for Distributed Practice	Ideas for Self-Directed Practice
•	•	•
•	•	•
•	•	•
•	•	•
•	•	•

DELIBERATE PRACTICE

We introduced the concept of deliberate practice earlier in this module, but we did not really explore what it means or how to encourage this type of practice in academic learning. Deliberate practice requires that each of the conditions noted previously be met (that is, it must be targeted, distributed, and self-directed), but it is a very specific type of practice. In fact, there are three types of practice: naïve, purposeful, and deliberate (Ericsson & Pool, 2016). As Ericsson and Pool noted, "We are drawing a clear distinction between purposeful practice—in which a person tries very hard to push himself or herself to improve—and practice that is both purposeful and informed. In particular, deliberate practice is informed and guided by the best performers' accomplishments and an understanding of what these expert performers do to excel. Deliberate practice is purposeful practice that knows where it is going and how to get there" (p. 1759).

Deans for Impact (2016) maintain there are five principles of deliberate practice as described in Figure 4.2. There is a visual of this model in Figure 4.3.

Figure 4.2   Principles of Deliberate Practice

	Principle	Description
1.	Push beyond one's comfort zone	Learning is challenging work, and deliberate practice requires that students push just beyond their current abilities. Students learn to accept the challenge of learning.
2.	Work toward well-defined, specific goals	Deliberate practice requires that efforts be aligned to specific, measurable goals that focus on a particular aspect of the skill or content rather than working toward broad general improvement.
3.	Focus intently on practice activities	Students must learn to direct their energy and focus on meaningful tasks rather than simply try to get them done as quickly as possible.
4.	Receive and respond to high-quality feedback	Students seek feedback and then use that feedback in the next iteration of their effort. In doing so, they monitor their progress toward successfully meeting the goal.
5.	Develop a mental model of expertise	Students have a clear picture of the skill that allows them to self-monitor and adjust their efforts.

Figure 4.3   The Five Principles of Deliberate Practice

Source: Deans for Impact (2016).

Some aspects of deliberate practice are the focus of other modules in this playbook, such as accepting the challenge of learning, monitoring progress, and seeking feedback. A point we'd like to make here, in the module focused on using tools to guide learning, is about the mental model of expertise. Students need to know what it will look like when they have learned something. To our thinking, this extends beyond the daily success criteria. Yes, those are important to motivate and engage students, but the purpose of using tools for learning extends beyond the individual day. Yes, we want students to practice each day, but we also want them to know what it looks like when they have mastered whatever it is they are learning.

> Students need to know what it will look like when they have learned or mastered something.

For example, Nancy's oldest grandson is interested in theater. When selected for a part, of course he practices his lines. And under the guidance of the director, the actors block the scenes and all learn their parts. But developing a mental model of expertise requires more than that. Nancy's grandson has studied actors that he finds relevant to his craft and notes what they do to have an impact on the audience. For example, he studied Jenna Ortega and her performances of Wednesday Addams. He noted the way she tilts her head down, how she doesn't blink, the way she moves her body, and how she seems to stare past you when talking. Jenna is but one of the actors he studies. The point is that he is developing a mental model of expertise—what it means to have an impact on your audience. The evidence on deliberate practice suggests that this is an important aspect of learning in any subject. By the way, did you note that we used the term *studied*? He studied Jenna. He did not just watch her performance. That's because studying is one of the clusters of skills that help students develop expertise.

STUDY SKILLS

Study skills are a constellation of competencies that allow students to acquire, record, organize, synthesize, remember, and use information (Hoover & Patton, 1995). And who wouldn't want students to be able to do those things? They are important in learning content, and they are transferable, allowing students to apply what they have learned in new situations.

Hattie (2009) suggested that study skills could be organized into three categories: *cognitive, metacognitive,* and *affective*. Combined, the effect size of study skills is 0.41.

Cognitive study skills usually involve a task, such as note taking or summarizing. Metacognitive study skills describe self-management, such as planning, monitoring, and recognizing when to use various cognitive strategies. Affective study skills involve motivation, agency, and self-concept. Figure 4.4 contains a table of study skills organized into these three categories. Hattie notes that teaching study skills in isolation can improve students' surface learning. We can learn "more" but not necessarily relate, apply, and more deeply understand the content. However, teaching study skills *within* content areas can improve deep learning. Elementary classrooms are ideal places to introduce and build study skills, as students generally have the same teacher for all subjects. Thus, teachers can integrate study skills into their science, social studies, and art lessons. As students move to middle and high school, teachers should be aware of and integrate study skills into their content area lessons. Importantly, there is no evidence that having a separate "study skills" class is going to ensure that students learn more or better.

Figure 4.4   Examples of Study Skills

Cognitive Study Skills	Metacognitive Study Skills	Affective Study Skills
• Note taking • Graphic organizers (creating and using) • Summarizing • Practice and rehearsal techniques (e.g., flashcards, mnemonics, memorization) • Rereading	• Planning for the task • Monitoring one's learning • Reviewing and revising corrected work • Self-assessment • Self-questioning	• Motivation to study • Structuring the environment to study • Belief in the usefulness of studying • Agency to influence one's learning • Willingness to solve problems • Managing stress and anxiety • Goal setting

For example, while learning the cardinal points of the compass, students in Michael Saunders's first-grade class were introduced to the mnemonic "never eat shredded wheat" to associate the directions in the correct order clockwise starting at the top. But as Mr. Saunders said to his class, "I really like shredded wheat, so I don't like to try to remember the directions with this saying. How about each table group come up with a different mnemonic that they can use to remember this information?" One of the groups came up with "never eat soggy waffles," and another group suggested "never eat shaved walrus," and still another said, "never eat salty worms."

The third-grade students in Hiroko Mayekawa's class used a free app called StudyBlue, which allows users to create flashcards with text, pictures, and audio. During their biomes investigation, students focused on diverse life forms from different environments. Ms. Mayekawa asked her students to create a series of flashcards so that they could remember the various biomes, the environmental conditions of those biomes, and the types of animals that lived in the environment. In doing so, she provided her students with a lot of options about what to include, and the app provided them with options for how to include their information. In creating the flashcards, students were studying the biomes. And in practicing with their flashcards, they were continuing to think about the content they were expected to learn.

Teaching study skills within content areas can improve deep learning.

PAUSE AND PONDER

What kinds of study skills have your students learned? Which do they apply? How do you or could you support their skills?

_____

_____

_____

_____

_____

_____

_____

_____

_____

_____

Many middle and high school programs teach students Cornell note taking, developed by a university law school dean to support candidates' studying habits for the bar exam (Pauk, 1962). Several note-taking frameworks work well for students, but Cornell notes are commonly used, as they apply across content areas and grades and allow students to develop a habit (see Figure 4.5). In this format, pages are divided into three sections. The major column is on the right, a minor column is on the left, and there is space at the bottom across the two columns. Students take notes in the major column but do not use the other two until they are ready to study. When they study their notes, they list key ideas in the minor column on the left and then summarize their notes at the bottom of the page.

Ninth-grade ethnic studies teacher Wren Washington makes sure her students understand that the value of their notes lies in what they do with them. "When I first started teaching, I was all about giving kids points for having a complete notebook," she chuckled. "I'd have notebook checks twice a quarter, and I'd see lots of really beautiful notes from some of my students. But I began to realize that there wasn't much connection between who was getting the maximum number of points on their notebook checks, and who was doing well on the tests I was giving."

Her conversations with students helped her understand that while many were putting their energy into making their notes, few looked back at them later. After doing some research on her own, she found a tool that proved to be useful for her students (Figure 4.6). This self-assessment of notes by Stahl et al. (1991) draws on the research on metacognitive awareness and requires students to examine their own note-taking habits. Ms. Washington introduced it to her students during the first week of classes and then spotlighted various aspects during subsequent class meetings during the first quarter. She started with the construction of the notes themselves, modeling effective note-taking behaviors during her lectures. Within a few weeks, she addressed how the notes should be used before and after class, even building in a few minutes of pre- and

Figure 4.5 Sample Cornell Notes Page

Cues	Notes
Use this area for key or main ideas. Phrase cues as questions. Fill this section in within 24 hours after class.	Record notes here during class or while reading. Consider using an outline format. Use meaningful abbreviations and symbols. Leave space to add additional information.
Summary	
Main ideas and major points are synthesized here. These are written during later review sessions.	

online resources Available for download at **resources.corwin.com/teachingstudentstodrivetheirlearning**

post-review time each day. "This proved to be the biggest game-changer for them," she said. "When they saw that reviewing and completing notes was valued in this class, they began to use them more often."

Figure 4.6 Assessment for Notes

	Never	Sometimes	Always
Pre-Lecture			
1. I read assignments and review notes before my classes.			
2. I come to class with the necessary tools for taking notes (pen and ruled paper).			
3. I sit near the front of the class.			
4. My notes are organized by subjects in a looseleaf notebook.			
5. I have a definite note-taking strategy.			
6. I adapt my note taking for different classes.			
Lecture			
1. I use my pen in note taking.			
2. I use only one side of the page in taking notes.			
3. I date each day's notes.			
4. I use my own words in writing notes.			
5. I use abbreviations whenever possible.			
6. My handwriting is legible for study at a later date.			
7. I can identify the main ideas in a lecture.			
8. I can identify details and examples for main ideas.			
9. I indent examples and details under the main ideas to show their relationship.			
10. I leave enough space to resolve confusing ideas in the lecture.			
11. I ask questions to clarify confusing points in the lecture.			

	Never	Sometimes	Always
Lecture			
12. I record the questions my classmates ask the lecturer.			
13. I am aware of instructor signals for important information.			
14. I can tell the difference between lecture and nonrelated anecdote.			
15. I take notes until my instructor dismisses class.			
Post-Lecture			
1. My notes represent the entire lecture.			
2. I review my notes immediately after class to make sure that they contain all the important points of the lecture and are legible.			
3. I underline important words and phrases in my notes.			
4. I reduce my notes to jottings and cues for studying at a later date.			
5. I summarize the concepts and principles from each lecture in a paragraph.			
6. I recite from the jottings and cues in the recall column on a weekly basis.			
7. I use my notes to draw up practice questions in preparation for examinations.			
8. I ask classmates for help in understanding confusing points in the lecture.			
9. I use my notes to find ideas that need further explanation.			
10. I am completely satisfied with my note taking in my courses.			
11. I can understand my notes when I study them later.			
12. I use the reading assignment to clarify ideas from the lecture.			

Source: Stahl et al. (1991). Reprinted with permission.

 TEACHER ACTIONS

Consider the following actions that reinforce or derail efforts to ensure that students know how to select tools that guide their learning. We have included blank lines for you to add your ideas.

Teacher Actions That Reinforce Students' Ability to Select Tools to Guide Their Learning	Teacher Actions That Derail Students' Ability to Select Tools to Guide Their Learning
• Introducing students to a range of tools • Providing opportunities for students to practice using tools • Structuring learning tasks so students can make choices about which tools to use • Asking students to reflect on the effectiveness of the strategy or tool that they chose	• Asking students to choose a tool without introducing and modeling those tools first • Preselecting all tools for students • Providing little opportunity for students to use tools or strategies that have been introduced • Discouraging mistakes in the tool selection process • Skipping the time to reflect on the process, and on the tools and strategies students selected
_____	_____
_____	_____
_____	_____
_____	_____
_____	_____
_____	_____
_____	_____
_____	_____
_____	_____
_____	_____
_____	_____
_____	_____
_____	_____
_____	_____
_____	_____

CONCLUSION

Teaching students to drive their learning includes helping them know where they're headed and providing tools for the journey. These tools are a set of metacognitive and cognitive strategies that propel their learning, especially when faced with challenge. It is important that students are taught about effective tools, but it's even more important that they come to understand a few things about these tools, namely

> Teaching students to drive their learning requires that they know where they're headed and that they have tools for the journey.

- Not all tools work for all problems.

- They have choice over which tools to use.

- They should replace tools that are not working.

Developing students' understanding of these principles requires that teachers provide them with multiple opportunities to try on learning tools. That means that learners need to make decisions about which strategies to select. In addition, as students increase their responsibility for their own learning, teachers must provide students with the means to assess their learning and then make adjustments to their learning plans, which might include the selection of new or different tools.

In this vein, study skills and deliberate practice become important considerations for teaching. It's not enough to "cover the content." Instead, teachers must focus on the ways in which people learn content, which includes practice and feedback.

NOTES

RETELLING PYRAMID

Create a pyramid of words, using the following prompts, that provides summarizing information. You're more likely to remember this information if you share with a peer.

1. One word that conveys an important topic in this module

2. Two words for tools or strategies that can be introduced to students

3. Three words for actions you can take based on this module

4. Four words that are key to your understanding

5. Five words that convey a goal you have based on this module

_____

_____　　_____

_____　　_____　　_____

_____　　_____　　_____　　_____

_____　　_____　　_____　　_____　　_____

Revisit the Text Impression summary you developed at the beginning of this module, and compare it to your current level of understanding. Where did your learning deepen?

_____

_____

_____

_____

_____

_____

_____

_____

_____

_____

_____

_____

_____

Using the traffic light scale, with red being not confident, yellow being somewhat confident, and green indicating very confident, how confident are you in your ability to

- Explore ideas for providing opportunities for students to practice selecting and using tools and strategies?

- Describe the principles of deliberate practice?

- Examine ideas for targeted, distributed, and self-directed practice?

- Identify examples of cognitive, metacognitive, and affective study skills?

5

LEARNERS MONITOR THEIR PROGRESS AND ADJUST THEIR LEARNING

We are learning to create opportunities for learners to monitor progress and adjust their learning.

SUCCESS CRITERIA

- I can foster habits of monitoring progress through reflective self-questioning.

- I can describe the characteristics of relevant and effective goals.

- I can explore the idea of co-constructing monitoring tools with students.

- I can explain how students learn to make adjustments in their learning.

The wellness industry has taught us how to monitor progress. There are any number of apps available for our smartphones, watches, and rings that provide us with data that we can use to monitor our progress toward a goal. The range of goals is pretty wide. Want to know how well you slept? There's a tool for that. Want to know how much exercise you completed and how many calories you expended? There's a tool for that, too. Do you want to know your heart rate and blood oxygen levels across the day? Again, there are some great tools to do that. Yes, we are awash with data that we *can* use to monitor progress toward our goals.

A few key points were contained in that last sentence. We do have data, but are they useful and actionable? Do we use the data to monitor and make changes, or do we just admire the problems presented in the data? And do we have goals or targets that are relevant for us so that we align the data with those goals? Each of these questions applies to academic learning and not just wellness. We do have a lot of data about students' learning, and there are several tools that teachers can use to make the evidence understandable and actionable for students.

> There are several tools that teachers can use to make the evidence understandable and actionable for students.

As you may have surmised by now, the factors contributing to students' learning to drive their learning are neither linear nor lockstep. Instead, they are interrelated. Think back to the modules about knowing where one is in the learning journey and understanding what one still needs to learn. Without those two, it's nearly impossible to monitor one's progress. We need goals (we call them learning intentions), and we need to know our current status. But, as we noted in those modules, simply knowing where you are and where you are going is not sufficient to ensure learning. In the last module we focused on the tools necessary to guide learning. In this module we focus on monitoring progress and then making adjustments if the data (in other words, evidence) suggest that you're not on track to achieve the goals.

TEXT IMPRESSION

Use the following words (in any order that works for you) to create an impression about what you think will be covered in this module.

self-questioning • transfer • progress • empowerment • academic planning • co-construction

_____

_____

_____

_____

_____

_____

_____

_____

_____

MONITORING REQUIRES LEARNERS TO SELF-QUESTION

Monitoring progress requires that we learn to ask ourselves questions. We must develop the skills of reflecting and using information to determine whether we are meeting our goals. The ability to question one's own understanding is a metacognitive strategy that assists in a learner's ability to self-regulate. We have discussed metacognition and self-regulation in earlier modules, so suffice to say that self-questioning provides students insight into what they know and do not know, and how they might move forward in their learning. Self-questioning can be useful as a study skill, especially in learning new material. For example, a valuable reading comprehension strategy is to teach students to pause and pose questions to themselves to check for understanding of what they have read (e.g., Joseph et al., 2016).

There is an optimal time for self-questioning, and it is not when we are learning the content (where building students' skills in evaluating evidence is more critical, with an effect size of 0.75) but when relating and going deeper in understanding. Here is where focusing on building skills to self-question (0.53), self-verbalize (0.53), self-explain (0.58), self-monitor (0.62), engage in self-judgment (0.66), and explore self-consequences (0.70) really make the difference (Hattie, 2023). Self-questioning for insight and reflection is a function of curiosity. Students who see their learning as something relevant and interesting to them are likely to be inclined to ask further questions about themselves and the topic they are studying. This is often associated with inquiry learning, although we think that term is limiting. Too often we have witnessed well-meaning educators launch into inquiry-based instruction, hoping to foster curiosity in their students. But curiosity and confusion are not one and the same.

Without adequate foundational, or surface, knowledge about the topic, students are more likely to be puzzled and dismissive when they lack the background knowledge they need actually to ask reflective questions. It's nearly impossible to contrive a creative solution when you know little about the topic or why you should care about it. This is why problem-based learning has such a poor overall effect (effect size 0.15); it's implemented too soon in the learning cycle.

However, when problem-based learning is introduced after students have deepened their learning on a topic, the effect size increases to 0.61. We'll put it another way: you need to know a lot to ask solid questions, explore inconsistencies, inquire, and solve problems. That is not to say that students must wait for self-questioning to emerge. The regular use of reflective prompts can activate the kind of questioning we want learners to use reflexively.

SELF-QUESTIONING TO REFLECT ON GOALS

The self-questioning tools we teach students must include an opportunity to reflect on their learning goals. After all, if they are engaging in all this metacognitive thinking, but not actually applying it to figure out where they're at and where they're headed, then we will have squandered a valuable opportunity to teach students to drive their learning. Student goal setting should be linked to the success criteria developed for the lesson, unit, or assignment. There are two elements to consider when it comes to goals. The first is the student's orientation—*why* they do what they do, and the second is goal setting—*what* they do to get there (Martin, 2013).

Goals can be oriented toward either mastery or performance. Martin explains, "Mastery orientation is focused on factors and processes such as effort, self-improvement, skill development, learning, and the task at hand. Performance orientation is focused more on demonstrating relative ability, social comparison, and outperforming others" (p. 353). In other words, it's the difference between saying, "I want to learn to speak Spanish" (mastery) rather than "I want to get an A in Spanish (performance)."

Although it may seem innocuous, a performance orientation often results in diminished academic risk taking and adventurousness (Martin et al., 2003). That's why we cringe when we see public displays of data that position one student against another. A chart that has everyone's reading level posted reinforces social comparisons. The focus shifts to standings. Instead, we want students to develop a mastery orientation positively associated with effort, learning, and improvement. With just a bit of shaping, that public data chart could report on each child's gains, for example, rather than on the individual's current reading level.

Goal setting should be about progress, not just outcomes.

Goal setting—what they do to get there—is the second element of the formula for helping students gauge their progress. Student goal setting has an effect size of 0.50, helping students become active participants in their own learning. The goals should be appropriately challenging (not too hard, not too boring), and should include regular check-ins that are motivating and direct a student's focus and attention. We do not subscribe to the belief that every student begins from the exact same place in their learning. Prior knowledge and present skill levels mean that every classroom will have a range of starting points. Goal setting should be about progress, not just outcomes. Solid goals meet four conditions:

- Specific in nature
- Challenging to the student
- Competitively self-referenced
- Based on self-improvement

NOTES

✎ NOTE TO SELF

What academic, school-related, or personal goal do you have for yourself? _____

_____

_____

- Why is this something you value? _____

_____

- What has your past performance been like? What has been your personal best so far? _____

_____

- How will achieving this goal benefit you? _____

_____

- How will you know you have been successful? _____

_____

- What might get in the way of you meeting this goal? _____

_____

- What do you need to achieve this goal? _____

_____

Resources		
Self	**Peers**	**Family**

Action steps to achieve this goal:

1.

2.

3.

Who is your accountability partner? _____

How often will you check in with your accountability partner? _____

Seventh-grade English teacher Simon Thompson assists his students in setting and reaching reading goals. Students are assessed at the beginning of the school year to measure their current reading levels, and Mr. Thompson meets individually with each student to discuss the results. Two students stand in contrast to one another. Bianca's results were consistent with current grade-level expectations, while Cassidy's were significantly lower. Mr. Thompson began each conference by discussing the meaning of the results, then moved the conversation to current reading habits. Not surprisingly, Bianca reads more frequently than her classmate Cassidy does. To help Bianca set her goals, he focused her attention on broadening the genres and topics she was reading. He posted her agreed-upon goal on the class goal chart: "My goal is to read two science fiction books, a collection of poetry, and three graphic novels this quarter."

He then met with Cassidy to discuss her results. Mr. Thompson also asked about reading habits and discovered that this student had not completed even one book the previous year. "It sounds like that's an excellent first goal for you. I can help you choose a book you're interested in, and then we'll meet to set the number of pages," he said. He and Cassidy met again two days later, after she had chosen a book by Kwame Alexander. "My brother showed me a video of him called 'Undefeated' and I liked it, so I thought I'd check him out." [You can view the video Cassidy watched at https://youtu.be/_cHIWtl8PNk.] Cassidy, whose passion is basketball, chose *The Playbook: 52 Rules to Aim, Shoot, and Score in This Game Called Life* (Alexander, 2017). "Plus, there are lots of pages that don't have lots of words on them, so I figured I could read it faster," she confessed. She agreed that 25 pages a week was reasonable.

By the following week, Cassidy had changed her goal. "I switched it to 35 pages 'cause I did 31 last week no sweat," she told Mr. Thompson. He changed her goal statement on the chart to reflect her new target. It now read, "I'm going to read *The Playbook*, 35 pages a week." Mr. Thompson said, "Looks like you're going for a PR [personal record]. That's how you get it done." She flipped to a page with a graphic and a large quote by Venus Williams and read it aloud to him: "'I don't focus on what I'm up against. I focus on my goal and I try to ignore the rest.'" Then she walked away smiling.

REVISITING "I CAN" STATEMENTS

We discussed the various ways that teachers can help students understand what successful learning looks like, such that they can answer the question: How do I know that I learned it? One of the common ways that this happens is by using "I can" statements. These statements can be converted from "I can" to "Can I . . . ?" questions, allowing students to monitor their progress and reflect on the amount of learning they have done.

First-grade teacher Ernesto Cruz has been using "I can" statements to assist young students in monitoring their progress. Mr. Cruz also posts "Can I?" questions at the end of lessons to encourage self-questioning. "Six-year-olds haven't developed the habit of self-inquiry," said the teacher, "so I help them with it." In the second quarter of the school year, he introduced several "Can I?" questions for students to use:

- Can I tell the order of events in a story?

- Can I explain the charts, diagrams, or maps used in an informational book?

- Can I compare new information I read about with what I already know?

- Can I write about what I have read?

"Each time I meet with a child to discuss a reading, we go back to these four questions," the teacher explained. "These represent the major skills I am teaching right now, and I want my students to be able to apply these across lots of things they read, not just a single story. By encouraging them to ask questions of themselves, they learn to check in with their own understanding. It's not just me informing them that they've learned something."

Similarly, science teacher Vanessa Gomez has her students self-assess against the "Can I?" questions, rating themselves on a scale of 1 (unsure) to 5 (confident) and then explaining their rationale for their response. For example, early in the school year in a lesson on the characteristics of life, students were asked to respond to the following: *Can I define homeostasis?*

Illeana rated herself a 3 and wrote,

> I rated myself a 3 because I need to look at my notes in order to define *homeostasis*. In class, we learned that homeostasis is "our body's tendency to maintain a stable internal environment" [reading from her notes], like body temperature, despite changes in the external environment. I will feel more confident defining *homeostasis* once we have more examples as a class and once I have more time to practice using this word in conversation.

Later in this same period, students were asked to respond to another success criterion: *Can I distinguish between positive and negative feedback?* Again, students rated themselves and provided an explanation for their ranking. In the process, they were developing the habit of monitoring their understanding and progressing toward the overall learning goals.

REVISITING SINGLE-POINT RUBRICS

Teachers can combine multiple "I can" statements to create a single-point rubric, first discussed in Module 2, which students can then use to monitor their progress (and, as we will see in the next module, they can also use these tools to seek feedback and provide feedback to their peers). For now, we'll focus on the use of single-point rubrics as a tool for students to monitor their own progress. Figure 5.1 contains the single-point rubric developed by second-grade teacher Justine Montiel as her class focused on subtracting. Note that there are several students' names in the rubric. As students explained their process for solving the problem, Ms. Montiel created or modified success criteria so that others would remember how their peers did this. In addition to specific strategies for subtracting, this tool includes the expectation that students can explain their own thinking and persevere as they work to find a solution.

Figure 5.1   Single-Point Rubric for Subtracting

Grow	Success Criteria	Glow
	I can use "Karly's Draw Everything Strategy."	
	I can use "Diego's Place Value Blocks Strategy" to decompose when subtracting.	
	I can use "Maria's Cross-Off Numbers Strategy."	
	I can explain how I decomposed a ten.	
	I can persevere by taking a deep breath and continuing my work or starting the problem over if I get lost in my work.	

online resources   Available for download at **resources.corwin.com/teachingstudentstodrivetheirlearning**

In this case, Ms. Montiel asks students to reflect on the areas where they need to grow versus where they are glowing. Shauntel noted that she was good at using Diego's Block Strategy, "but I don't know about crossing them off. But when I can't do it, I get mad and tell Kiana to help me." Kiana added, "I need to grow in the explaining. I can do it, but I get mixed up when I tell someone else about it."

PAUSE AND PONDER

Self-regulation, planning, and organizing can help students learn to drive their learning. We have provided several tools that can help students develop these skills as they monitor their progress. How do you envision creating these opportunities in your classroom?

_____

_____

_____

_____

_____

_____

_____

_____

_____

CO-CONSTRUCTING MONITORING TOOLS WITH STUDENTS

Emily Licona asked a group of students to be seated at the table in the center of the classroom. A few days earlier, Ms. Licona had recruited volunteers for this fishbowl activity. This group of students had practiced their scripts and were ready to showcase how an effective collaborative discussion looked and sounded, and the other students were ready to observe. Ms. Licona announced that they were going to carefully watch this group interact and note what made this collaborative conversation so effective.

The students watched their peers as they engaged in a collaborative discussion about a page in the novel *Ghost* by Reynolds (2016). The teacher then asked the class to generate a list of things they noticed about what members of the group did and said that made the discussion work.

Sebastian noticed that each group member had the text in front of them and that there were annotations on the text. Several students noticed that after Jessica asked a question, students took turns responding. Marla noticed that when one member of the group had not had the opportunity to speak, they were invited into the conversation with, "Javier, what do you think?" Richard noticed that after group members responded, Charlie often asked, "What in the text makes you think that?"

Ms. Licona recorded the responses from students. In their groups, students worked on categorizing their observations. The result was a rubric that was designed by the students that showed exactly was success looked like. They could use it in monitoring their progress as they interacted with their peers (see Figure 5.2). Ms. Licona added sentence frames they could use to engage with their peers.

Figure 5.2   Group Talk Rubric

Grow	Success Criteria	Glow
	I can come to the discussion prepared (text annotated, answers and questions ready).	
	I can take turns speaking. "Who would like to go first?" "I'll start." "_____, what do you think?"	
	I can provide evidence from the text to support my answer. "I think _____, because in paragraph _____, it says. . . ." "What in the text makes you think that?"	
	I can listen and build on the ideas of others. "Can you say that again, please?" "I agree/disagree with _____, because _____."	

CONNECTIONS

Not all content and points in the school year will be conducive to this approach, and there are several other tools that students can use to monitor their progress. When might co-construction of the tools useful for monitoring progress be appropriate?

_____

_____

_____

_____

_____

What impact might co-constructing monitoring tools have on student motivation for learning?

_____

_____

_____

_____

_____

What impact might co-constructing monitoring tools have on clarity of the success criteria?

_____

_____

_____

_____

_____

What impact might co-constructing monitoring tools have on students' ability to set goals?

_____

_____

_____

_____

_____

PLANNING AND ORGANIZING TO ADJUST LEARNING

Self-regulation is evidenced as students learn to plan and make adjustments in the actions they are taking to learn. Young children can be asked to plan for simple tasks, such as considering which materials they will need to complete an assignment, or what kinds of clothing are needed for different weather conditions. Academic planning requires a level of organization that is essential for completing more complex tasks, such as writing. Effective writers plan their writing using various strategies, including brainstorming to list ideas and freewriting to put them into motion. Freewriting is a timed writing practice used to begin to convert lists to more connected texts.

When his writing stalls, ninth-grade student Kolby uses a freewriting technique he first learned in middle school. His teacher introduced him to the practice of first listing topics and ideas for a paper through a five-minute brainstorming session, and following this with an additional ten minutes of freewriting. "My goal is to use as many of the words on my brainstorming list as I can, and to write at least 100 words," Kolby said. "I don't get too focused on making sure I used all the ideas on my list, or even if I wrote 100 words or not," he explained. "But it definitely gets me going, and I'm not just keeping staring at a blank screen."

Fourth-grade student Riley uses planning for her reading. "Last year my teacher taught us how to first skim a reading to look at all the headings. That gives me information about what I'm going to read about." Her classmate Israel added, "Sometimes I turn [the headings] into questions." Other planning comes in the form of thinking about the time needed. Eleventh-grade student Marcus is reading *David Copperfield* in his British Literature course:

> We read *Silas Marner* last year, so I know that it takes time to work through a Dickens novel. There's like a jillion characters. We're reading it like it was originally written, in serial form. I've got Chapters 25–27 to read and be ready to discuss on Thursday. I put it in my calendar to block out time to read and annotate. Dude got paid by the word. Did ya know?

Riley, Israel, and Marcus have something in common. They are not simply consuming information, but actually strategically planning for how they will understand it, especially as they confront an obstacle to their progress or anticipate a challenging task. In other words, they adjust their learning. Riley skims and scans, Israel converts headings to questions, and Marcus uses time management and annotation in his reading. Their planning in turn serves as a way to organize their thinking, which is a second critical metacognitive skill. When we refer to *organization,* we don't mean the physical environment (although that is a good study skill), but rather to build schema, which is the mental structure you use to frame a network of related knowledge.

For example, when you read about Marcus's assignment to read David Copperfield, it may have triggered elements of your own schema. *What do I know about Charles Dickens? Do I know why this was his favorite novel? What do I know about mid-19th-century life? What do I know about newspaper serials of the time? What experiences have I had in wading through a really long book?* The fact that you can retrieve this information speaks to your mental organization of all this related information. It also reflects your ability to self-question, monitor, and adjust your learning as needed. That's one reason note-taking guides and concept maps can be so useful for building schema. They foster mental organization of information into categories, so the learner can retrieve it more easily. Marcus's use of annotation is a great study skill precisely because it assists the learner in organizing information to build schema.

COLLABORATING AS A WAY TO ADJUST LEARNING

Remember Ms. Licona? She taught her students to monitor their success while engaged with peers in collaborative discussions. She knows that learning is largely a social endeavor, and opportunities to hear what others are thinking as they try ideas on for size and work toward consensus can be of immense value. Participation in small group discussions can allow learners to express their own thoughts, especially as new insight is sometimes borne from trying to explain something to someone else. The effect size for students who regularly work together collaboratively and cooperatively is 0.42.

But we think that there is more possible than just cooperation when it comes to students making adjustments to their learning based on where they are in their learning journey. We have described this as *collective student efficacy*, which requires that we develop students' beliefs that by working with other people, they will learn more. Students with high levels of collective efficacy

- Value the contributions of their peers.

- Know that their opinions and ideas are worthy of consideration.

- Display confidence in the team's collective ability.

- Believe that their time together is useful.

- Understand that they are each integral to the overall task completion.

- Learn more as a result of their interactions.

- Use their individual (or, as we call them, "I") skills as well as collaborative (or, as we call them, "we") skills (Hattie et al., 2021, p. 13).

> When students learn to routinely ask questions of one another, the effect is that the habit of self-questioning gets baked into peer interactions.

Students working in pairs or small groups must learn to listen carefully, consider the ideas of others, present their own, and come to consensus. In doing so, they make adjustments to their learning. These are not inconsequential actions; they are honed over a lifetime of experiences working with others. When students learn to routinely ask questions of one another, the effect is that the habit of self-questioning gets baked into peer interactions. Students begin to use these opportunities to monitor their own understanding and make adjustments to their thinking as they reach consensus or resolve contradictions.

THINK-OUTSIDE-THE-BOX QUESTIONS

When students learn to think together and individually, both critically and creatively, they develop intellectual habits that foster the transfer of learning. Transfer of learning is the ultimate measure of learning, as students are able to apply skills, concepts, and knowledge in increasingly new and unique situations.

These intellectual habits can be fostered through elaborative questioning processes that cause students to consider what is known, seek patterns, speculate, draw conclusions, and arrive at creative solutions. Figure 5.3 features a flowchart and sample questions that student teams can utilize as they work through challenging texts and problems. These think-outside-the-box questions, adapted from the work of King (1992), are not isolated questions to be selected off a list, but rather provide the discussion group with a map of how to move their thinking forward through each stage.

Figure 5.3   Think-Outside-the-Box Questions

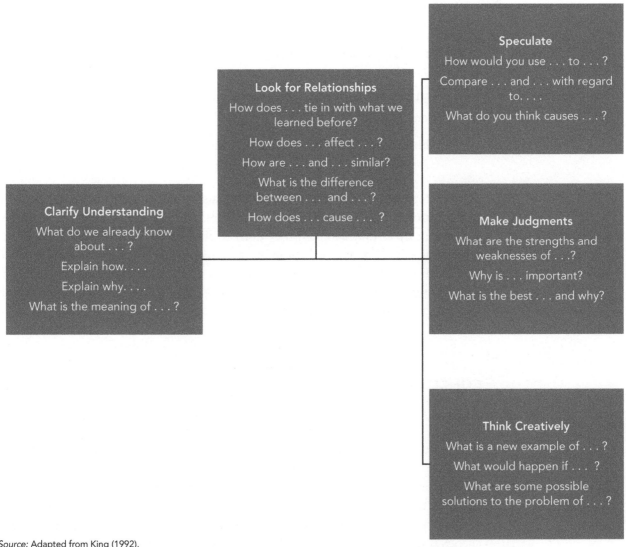

Source: Adapted from King (1992).

Natalya Alvarez-Gallagher developed her own version of think-outside-the-box questions to foster habits for her third graders. While her students solve rich mathematical tasks together, Ms. Alvarez-Gallagher intermittently pauses the action to pose questions. These extended math tasks often take 15 minutes or more and have lots of text and data for the students to wade through. "I call them 'think breaks,' and I post a question for all of them to see," she explained. "They stop what they're doing to check in with each other, especially so they can monitor how it's going, or if they have overlooked something."

One mathematical task these students were solving involved developing a plan for planting a garden that would allow for the largest number of plants to be planted within a fixed area. The students needed to determine the best plan among the three they had been given. They also needed to select among several choices of seeds, each of which varied in the area needed for optimal growth. At varying points throughout the task, Ms. Alvarez-Gallagher paused their thinking with a series of questions:

- **Clarify your understanding**: What do we know about this problem? What are we being asked to do? (*Question posed after a two-minute initial review of the task.*)

- **Look for relationships**: How is this problem similar to what we have been learning in math? (*Question posed four minutes into the activity.*)

- **Speculate**: What are we sure of? What mistakes should we watch out for? (*Question posed ten minutes into the activity.*)

- **Make judgments**: Is there something we can eliminate? Is there an idea that seems best? (*Question posed 12 minutes into the activity.*)

- **Think creatively**: How would our answer change if we had fewer seeds? (*Question posed at the end of the activity.*)

Ms. Alvarez-Gallagher said that she has seen a shift in her students' thinking as the year has progressed. "I always have some students who are in a rush to solve the problem as quickly as they can, and they don't really involve the other members of the group," she said. "These timed questions are causing them to slow down and listen to others. It's also giving them a way to check their own thinking. I've also started posting these same questions on their math assessments as a reminder that math is about thinking, not being a calculator," said the teacher.

CONCLUSION

Students who drive their learning are empowered learners.

Teaching students to drive their learning must include opportunities for students to engage in reflective self-questioning, and by extension to do so with peers. Teachers can create these opportunities for learners to reflect on their learning and thereby build habits. Habits such as these invite students to monitor their own progress. Unfortunately, too many students are lulled into passivity, because they have learned to rely on the teacher, and not themselves, to gauge their progress. The co-development of mastery goals shifts the responsibility of learning, as students are invited to take charge. If this sounds a bit like student empowerment, it is. Students who drive their learning are empowered learners.

TEACHER ACTIONS

Consider the following actions that reinforce or derail efforts to ensure that students know their current level of understanding. We have included blank lines for you to add your ideas.

Teacher Actions That Reinforce Students' Ability to Monitor Their Progress and Adjust Their Learning	Teacher Actions That Derail Students' Ability to Monitor Their Progress and Adjust Their Learning
• Intentionally building moments into a lesson that allow for students to reflect on their progress • Changing "I can" statements into "Can I" questions, so students can reflect on what they have learned and set their next goal • Explicitly teaching and modeling planning and organizing strategies • Structuring tasks so that students are required to interact with one another	• Expecting students to just know how to write goals for themselves • Evaluating student learning without helping students monitor their own progress • Asking students to engage in problem-based learning before students have the foundational skills and knowledge needed to apply their learning • Shying away from challenging students with complex tasks

RETELLING PYRAMID

Create a pyramid of words, using the following prompts, that provides summarizing information. You're more likely to remember this information if you share with a peer.

1. One word that conveys an important topic in this module

2. Two words for an opportunity to support students in engaging in self-questioning

3. Three words for actions you can take based on this module

4. Four words that are key to your understanding

5. Five words that convey a goal you have based on this module

_____

_____   _____

_____   _____   _____

_____   _____   _____   _____

_____   _____   _____   _____   _____

Revisit the Text Impression summary you developed at the beginning of this module, and compare it to your current level of understanding. Where did your learning deepen?

_____

_____

_____

_____

_____

_____

_____

_____

_____

_____

_____

_____

_____

Using the traffic light scale, with red being not confident, yellow being somewhat confident, and green indicating very confident, how confident are you in your ability to

- Foster habits of monitoring progress through reflective self-questioning?

- Describe the characteristics of relevant and effective goals?

- Explore the idea of co-constructing monitoring tools with students?

- Explain how students learn to make adjustments in their learning?

6

LEARNERS SEEK FEEDBACK
and Recognize That Errors Are Opportunities to Learn

LEARNING INTENTION

We are learning to create opportunities for learners to seek feedback and recognize that errors are opportunities to learn.

SUCCESS CRITERIA

- I can explain empathetic feedback.

- I can describe the five aspects of the GREAT feedback framework.

- I can identify the four types of feedback.

- I can create feedback opportunities and model seeking feedback.

- I can describe the learning outcomes of the four possible learning events.

Students who reliably gauge their own progress not only seek but are receptive to receiving copious amounts of feedback. As we noted in the last module, they develop a feedback loop by engaging in reflective self-questioning and taking action, thereby becoming more metacognitively aware. In addition to monitoring their own progress, students who drive their learning seek feedback—they do not wait passively for feedback. Peers are an important, yet often untapped, source of feedback, particularly when students engage in peer critiques. And teachers are a major source for feedback. But not all feedback is useful. First, it needs to be timely. It's remarkable how quickly feedback gets stale. In addition, it should be specific and actionable, meaning that students can apply the feedback to revise their work. Saving your very best feedback for the summative assignment is a waste of your time and theirs if students don't have an opportunity to act upon it.

> Students who drive their learning seek feedback; they do not wait passively for feedback.

But just because teachers provide copious amounts of feedback does not mean that students hear, understand, or can act on this feedback. Many consider feedback to be a "cost"—they have to do more or do the work again; it was not good enough. It becomes a skill for them to "not hear" feedback, as it is for us adults. Also, too often feedback comes at the end of a piece of work, and there is no opportunity to act on any feedback—so why bother listening to it? And even when students "hear" the feedback, do they understand it? It is a fascinating exercise to ask students to make notes on the feedback they receive, so you as the teacher can "hear" how they understand your feedback. (Be prepared—some will note nothing despite a half page of your comments—this is feedback to you that your feedback was not received or understood.)

Finally, can the student act on the feedback, and does the student do so? Like the proverbial tree in the forest, if your feedback is not acted on, was it truly feedback? Teaching students how to hear, understand, and act on feedback can be critical, as it is for you to hear, understand, and see whether your feedback is acted upon. When we are asked what good feedback is, the simple answer is that good feedback is the feedback you provided that was acted upon.

With all the emphasis on feedback, it is important to note that the ultimate arbiter of its usefulness is the receiver, not the giver. The student determines whether the feedback is understandable, meaning the teacher must be attuned to feedback language. If a student doesn't understand the feedback a teacher gives, then it isn't useful. Period.

Perceptions about feedback are influenced by cultural and personal factors specific to the learner, to be sure. Gee (2014), in a study of the effects of teacher feedback on writing, noted that there are three main effects: "saying, doing, and being" (p. 3). The feedback we provide to students tends to be consciously focused on what is said and what we want them to do next. But as educators we may not always perceive its effect on student identity—the "being" dimension of Gee's feedback frame. The notion of *feedback literacy*, in which teachers and students understand the elements, effects, and purposes of feedback, has been forwarded by many researchers (Ketonen et al., 2020; Mandouit & Hattie, 2023; Sutton, 2012).

Consistent with the dimensions of developing students' ability to drive their learning, Carless and Boud (2018) outlined four dimensions of student feedback literacy:

- **Appreciating feedback** as a means to strengthen their learning, while also understanding that feedback comes in a variety of forms and sources. In addition, they know that storing and returning to the feedback will enhance their efforts

- **Making judgments** so they can accurately judge their own work and the work of peers, and participate in peer critique opportunities

- **Managing affect** to avoid being defensive, and make it a habit to seek feedback from others

- **Taking action** is a product of the first three, in that students must act upon the feedback and have a repertoire of strategies to do so.

However, the effectiveness of developing *student* feedback literacy is balanced by the *teacher's* feedback literacy. Carless and Winstone (2023) studied this interplay and noted that teacher feedback literacy is expressed through the following deliberate actions:

- A design dimension that focuses on designing feedback processes for student uptake and enabling student evaluative judgment

- A pragmatic dimension that addresses how teachers manage the compromises inherent in disciplinary and institutional feedback practices

- A relational dimension that represents the interpersonal side of feedback exchanges

This last element is a major factor and speaks to the inherent importance of the student's positive relationship with the teacher. Relational trust is an important element of teacher credibility. And examination by Zumbrunn et al. (2016) of middle and high school students' perceptions of feedback about their writing noted that students' relationship to the teacher had a mediating effect. While most of the student respondents (80%) said they liked receiving feedback about their writing, 20% did not. Among those who had a negative perception, 65% of student comments disregarded the source of the feedback (the teacher) and expressed indifference to the value of feedback for them:

- "If I'm happy with my writing, their opinion doesn't matter."
- "It's annoying."
- "I don't really care."
- "I'm really not interested in getting feedback."
- "Some teachers are mean."
- "I don't like writing and [teachers] are really critical, so I just say whatever and keep writing."

> Feedback should help students become more consciously aware of what they are doing, their decisions for doing so, and what problem-solving strategies and processes they can use to correct, revise, or improve their work.

A related study of elementary students drew similar conclusions. Children drew pictures of themselves writing in the classroom and discussed their perceptions. Some students' negative perceptions cited isolation from the teacher, and those students stated that they experienced anxiety about or physical or emotional pain associated with their writing (Zumbrunn et al., 2017).

At its best, feedback should help students become more consciously aware of what they are doing, their decisions for doing so, and what problem-solving strategies and processes they can use to correct, revise, or improve their work. It isn't enough to provide instruction on strategies; we must link them to the self-regulation the learners can exercise to gauge their progress and move forward. Our own feedback literacy is the link between the two.

-------------------•
Feedback must be seen
as a two-way street.

TEXT IMPRESSION

Use the following words (in any order that works for you) to create an impression about what you think will be covered in this module.

praise • feedback received • empathetic • monologue • capacity building • help seeking • unproductive success

_____

_____

_____

_____

_____

_____

_____

_____

_____

_____

_____

_____

_____

Feedback has been described as the most underutilized instructional approach teachers have at their disposal. Teachers will often say that they know feedback is useful, but they offer *useful* feedback surprisingly infrequently, with most incidents consisting of general praise of a nonspecific nature ("You've done a fantastic job!"), and usually only one or two sentences in length (Voerman et al., 2012). It truly is a lost opportunity as well, since the effect size of feedback is 0.62. Perhaps it is effective because it encapsulates many of the sound approaches detailed throughout this playbook. The purpose of feedback should remain constant—to progressively close the gap between present and desired performance or learning. To do so, the teacher and the student must have

- The ability to determine the present level of performance (Module 2)

- A clear and shared understanding of the learning intentions and success criteria (Module 3)

- Strategies and processes that can be put into action (Module 4)

- Ways to gauge the next steps to move forward (Module 5)

Importantly, feedback must be seen as a two-way street. Teachers provide feedback to students and in turn gain feedback from students. After all, students' work, understandings, questions, misconceptions, and errors are all feedback to us about our performance. Therefore, feedback should not be viewed as a one-way transmission model, but as one that operates dynamically between teacher and student.

NOTES

CONNECTIONS

We noted the overall effect size of feedback at 0.62. But there are many aspects of feedback that have different effect sizes. Note each of these and how you might use them in your classroom.

Aspect of Feedback and Effect Size	Definition	How I Might Use This . . .
Feedback from tests (ES = 0.48)	Feedback is given based on testing; using evidence from the test to give feedback	
Using reinforcement and cues for feedback (ES = 0.92)	Positive and negative reinforcement and cues to advance to next steps in learning	
Feedback using technology (ES = 0.61)	Using technology tools to deliver feedback for students	

A MODEL FOR FEEDBACK

There are several factors that can strengthen feedback (Wisniewski et al., 2020):

- It is especially good for cognitive and physical tasks, but less so for motivation and behavior.

- Feedback that includes information about the task, processing the task, and self-regulation is better than feedback that is simply corrective.

- Feedback in oral or written form is equally useful.

However, a common misunderstanding is that effectiveness is all about feedback given—in other words, the more the better. It's really about feedback *received* by the learner. And the best way for students to receive feedback is to teach them how to ask for it, and then allow them to ask for it. Feedback isn't better just because you spend more time providing it. Most of these feedback conversations take only a few minutes to complete. But regular doses of great feedback can provide the teacher and the student with learning opportunities while fueling a positive relationship.

PAUSE AND PONDER

Consider the times in your own life when you received feedback you dismissed. Perhaps you didn't have a trusting relationship with the person who delivered it, and you were suspicious of their motives. Or perhaps you didn't think the person was a credible source of information on the topic. Even if the feedback was accurate, you likely failed to act on it. Write some notes about this experience so you can avoid that in your classroom.

_____

_____

_____

_____

_____

_____

_____

_____

_____

THE GREAT FEEDBACK MODEL

We looked at models both inside and outside of education that would capture best practices informed by feedback research. We found one in the GREAT model developed by LarkApps, a team productivity and engagement company that specializes in supporting businesses whose employees work remotely but collaborate regularly. They note that empathetic feedback is key to high performance precisely because it attends to the quality of the relationship. The GREAT feedback framework consists of five facets:

- **Growth oriented:** It signals one's intention as constructive and focused on improvement rather than criticism.
- **Real:** The feedback is honest, targeted, and actionable; not holistic, vague, or false praise.
- **Empathetic:** It combines critique with care and a quest for mutual understanding.
- **Asked for:** It encourages the receiver to ask questions and seek feedback.
- **Timely:** Feedback gets stale fast, so you want to make sure it is delivered soon.

Let's take each one of those dimensions and play it out with a student. As you read the following section, consider it in the light of feedback literacy on the part of the teacher and the student. The goal is to ensure that students know where they are going next in their learning and how to get there.

Growth Oriented

Start with your intention to provide feedback such that it meets this first condition. Ask yourself, are you ready to provide growth-producing feedback, or are you still in a place of criticizing? If you are not yet ready to move from criticism, it's not time for feedback. For instance, middle school English teacher Taylor Hayden sits next to a student and begins, "Saylor, I noticed that you've been working on your essay revision, and you added your name to the list of people ready for feedback. Is this a good time for some feedback so that you can make the most of your additions?"

> Real feedback includes rich information that provides the learner with details about what to start, continue, and change.

When we asked students what they understood by feedback, their answers were pretty consistent. For students, feedback is the answer to the question "Where to next"?

Feedback From Student Perspective

Where have I done well?	Where can I improve?	How do I improve?	What do I do next time?
• Indicates where done well	• Error flagging —what—where?	• Elaborate ideas	• Next time . . .
• Understanding	• Corrections and corrective	• How to improve	• Critical thinking
• Positive emotions: encouraged, confident		• Suggestions/ examples/tips	• Ability to self-regulate
		• Explain errors	

Real

Information-rich feedback provides the learner with details about what to start, continue, and change. This information needs to be actionable and honest. All of our students have received false praise, and it's not helpful. Real feedback is also not only corrective ("This one's right and that one's wrong"). Rather, it gives the learner information about the task, the process, and perhaps their self-regulation. The teacher begins by stating something to continue. "You're effectively showing your thinking on paper with your thesis statement. One thing to start doing is to restate one important idea at the beginning of each of the next paragraphs. One thing to stop is to say the thesis statement again at the end of each paragraph, because it's not necessary for your reader. I have to add, your persistence in making this a polished piece really shows." It's important not to overwhelm the learner with more feedback they can process at a given time. Notice that the teacher focused on the thesis statement and how it plays out in subsequent paragraphs.

Again, we note the difference between effective feedback at the task level and at the deeper level. Feedback focused on correct-incorrect response is more powerful at the task level. The example above includes feedback that supports students at the deeper level of learning.

Empathetic

It's easy for feedback to be reduced to lots of "you" directives. Be sure that the feedback also contains "I" messages that foster empathetic listening, as the evidence is that we listen more effectively when someone uses this pronoun. This can reduce that initial defensive clench that might otherwise shut down the conversation before it has begun. "When I read your draft essay, I can already see how effective your thesis is. For me as a reader, the reminders about your thesis help me to join you in your argument," says the teacher. The message is to show the student you have heard what they are aiming to say or do, and this increases the probability that students will then listen and understand the subsequent feedback.

Adding some "we" statements to the feedback can demonstrate for students that their teacher (or peers as they learn to incorporate the GREAT feedback model) empathizes with them and their learning journey. For example, Ms. Hayden adds, "We can review a few examples from other writers together if that's helpful, or we could record some peer responses and listen to them together."

Asked For

Effective feedback is a dialogue, not a monologue. Simply blasting a student with lots of feedback isn't likely to foster a relationship. The content of the feedback is based on what the student is asking about. The students in Ms. Hayden's class add their names to an electronic database when they are ready for feedback and include items that they'd like to focus on during the conversation.

> The content of the feedback needs to be based on what the student is asking about.

After providing microfeedback, invite the student to ask questions. "What questions do you have for me? Is there anything you're confused about?" says Ms. Hayden. Saylor responds, "I thought we were supposed to restate the idea in each paragraph. I know it's on the rubric for this essay. Where do I restate my thesis?" The student's response now becomes feedback to the teacher, who recognizes that for this student, the instruction wasn't clear. The two of them discuss further restating the thesis in the concluding paragraph of the essay.

Timely

This final dimension of feedback doesn't come in the form of a statement, but rather in its relationship to time. As novice teachers, we made the rookie error of saving our best feedback for the end of an assignment, only to witness students checking for the grade and discarding the rest. Imagine what the effect would have been if the conversation between Saylor and the teacher hadn't happened until the final draft was submitted. Make sure that the feedback occurs at a time when it remains actionable.

✏️ NOTE TO SELF

In addition to avoiding directives and using "I" statements, several teacher actions increase the sense of empathy on the part of the receiver of the feedback. Consider each of these actions, and identify ways that you could incorporate them into a feedback session with students.

Empathetic Feedback Component	Definition	How I Can Use This . . .
Start with success.	Tell them one thing that they did well.	
Make it manageable.	Use microfeedback to focus on one important but small thing at a time.	
Recruit the receiver.	Switch to a "we" statement following each microfeedback statement.	
Create a culture of appreciation.	Thank the receiver for participating, listening, acting upon, or something else.	
Seek your own feedback.	Obtain feedback about your feedback—the impact, usefulness, or ways to improve.	

TYPES OF FEEDBACK

Remember that the usefulness of the feedback is in the eye of the beholder. Therefore, feedback should address the three major questions learners have (Hattie & Timperley, 2007):

1. Where am I going?

2. How am I going there?

3. Where will I go next?

The first question is addressed through the learning intentions and success criteria. Knowing what success looks like allows students to strive with the teacher to achieve these goals. If the goal, for example, is to write a detailed explanation of factors leading to the failure of the Fukushima Daiichi nuclear reactor in 2011, omitting information from prior safety studies would be an error that would need to be corrected.

That's exactly what chemistry teacher Dennis Eagleton did when he met with a student Sharla to discuss her first draft. "I read your draft yesterday and noted the questions you asked about for feedback. You're off to a great start," he began. "Let's look at this together so we can figure out how best to support your next draft." After identifying strengths in her initial report ("you provided an account of the disaster at the beginning of the paper, which set the context for understanding its magnitude"), he turned his attention to the checklist for the report. "What's missing for me so far is information about any safety concerns prior to the disaster."

> Make sure that the feedback occurs at a time when it remains actionable.

Mr. Eagleton then went on to address the second question, which concerns using strategies to address discrepancies. "So let's talk for a few minutes about where we might locate this information. I was thinking that maybe making a list of places to check out is going to prevent you from forgetting the ideas we brainstorm." He and Sharla spend a few minutes discussing possibilities, including checking the Japanese Nuclear Safety Commission and International Atomic Energy Agency websites for information. Because the students in his class were researching nuclear disasters from around the world, including Chornobyl and Three Mile Island, he had curated several appropriate resources on his course learning management system (LMS). However, Sharla had overlooked these resources when developing her initial draft.

Mr. Eagleton then shifted his focus to the third question, addressing Sharla's next steps. "What's next for you? It's important that you have a plan. What two or three things are you going to do?"

Sharla offered, "Well, I've got some reading to do, looking for any safety reports. Once I write up that part, I'm going to have someone else who's not working on Fukushima read it just to make sure it makes sense." And, smiling, she said, "I guess I need to use the checklist a little better, too. Thanks, Mr. E!" With that, Sharla headed back to her research team.

We don't mean to oversimplify feedback by reducing it to a three-step process, but rather to use the process as a frame to make the feedback as useful as possible. For many students, if there is no "where-to-next" feedback, then they often say they received no feedback. In reality, there are four types of feedback that can be incorporated into the model of providing feedback (Hattie & Timperley, 2007). Depending on the student and the need, feedback may address one or more of four different types. These types of feedback are typically interwoven throughout the feedback process.

The first type is feedback about the task or product. This type of feedback is sometimes called *corrective feedback,* as it provides information about the accuracy or completeness of the assignment. Mr. Eagleton used this type of feedback to highlight what Sharla had included (context) and what she had omitted (safety concerns prior to the event).

Mr. Eagleton also provided a second type of feedback, which was about processes. In his case, he focused on strategies, especially identifying possible resources for her. The teacher also included a third type of feedback, which concerns self-regulation. He asked Sharla about what she would do to support her own critique of her written draft, and she noted that she would consult the checklist a bit more closely and have a peer read her next version to see if it made sense.

Notice that he did not make the mistake of confining his feedback to the fourth type of feedback, which is about the person receiving the feedback. These comments often take the form of praise, usually general and vague, and have very little impact on learning with an effect. Telling Sharla, "You're off to a good start!" without any further information is not helpful to her and would have indicated that the teacher himself hadn't thought deeply about the student's work. We are not suggesting that students should never be praised. But self-efficacy is about confidence in one's capacity and capability. Self-efficacy is drawn from knowing about the specifics, including what has already been accomplished and what should occur next.

We mentioned before that feedback goes both ways, and Mr. Eagleton is attuned to this concept. He kept an informal tally of the errors he saw most commonly, so he could plan for some reteaching the following day. He told the class,

> I talked to several of you who hadn't made use of the checklist before submitting your work to the LMS. Tonight I'm going to change the online protocol so that you can submit a completed checklist with your draft. That should help. I'm also going to update the resources I have online. Several students mentioned great resources they used that were not on the LMS. I made a list, and I'm going to add them so that others can use them. I'll review the new resources at the beginning of class tomorrow.

MODELING SEEKING FEEDBACK

In Ms. Garcia's fourth-grade class, students are learning to internalize the idea that feedback is something to be excited about. She decides to distribute a survey to her students, so she can seek their feedback (Figure 6.1). She tells students that she would appreciate their honesty, because she is excited to have a goal to work on for the quarter. She tells the students, "You have all chosen goals for this first quarter, and I want a goal too. I am always trying to be a better teacher, and I need your help deciding an area I want to work to improve. I have written some questions I would like you to answer."

The next day, Ms. Garcia announced, "After reviewing the surveys, I am so excited to reveal what my goal this quarter will be. I am going to learn more about how to give more practice work that is more helpful and meaningful. I am so excited to take on this goal, and I appreciate the feedback from this class."

Figure 6.1   Feedback for the Teacher

	No 1	Sometimes 2	Yes 3
1. My teacher cares about me.			
2. Every day I get a chance to work with my peers.			
3. My teacher wants to get to know me.			
4. My teacher gives me enough practice to be able to do the work on my own.			
5. My teacher is organized and ready to teach me.			
6. My teacher is excited to teach us.			
7. I feel like I am in control of my learning.			
8. I get to talk to my teacher every day.			
9. My teacher helps me when I need it.			
10. My teacher gives me practice work that helps me learn.			

online resources Available for download at **resources.corwin.com/teachingstudentstodrivetheirlearning**

MODELING MAKING MISTAKES

At Lakeside Elementary, principal Judy Harper sends out a weekly school video message that teachers show in their classrooms on Monday morning. The weekly message is a great way for students to hear the news for the week and includes a weekly question that students discuss. First-grade teacher Kenneth Youth apologized to his class Tuesday morning for forgetting to play the video yesterday in class. It was the third week in a row that he showed the video on Tuesday after forgetting to show the video on Monday. He said, "I keep making this mistake, and I know that when I make a mistake, it is a chance for me to do something different and learn from my mistake. So, I have an idea."

Mr. Youth showed the class five magnetized pictures of the principal, and he added those pictures to the Monday box of the classroom calendar on the wall. "Now we have a reminder to play our Monday video! Remember that making mistakes means that you are about to learn something new or come up with a great idea!" Later in the week, Principal Harper walked into the room and noticed several pictures of herself on the class calendar.

"Why is my face on the calendar?" she laughed.

Trinity, a first-grade student, spoke up, "Because Mr. Youth made a mistake and mistakes give you great ideas!"

Students want to make improvements, but do not usually know how to ask for specific feedback. The use of success criteria or the single-point rubrics discussed in an earlier module supports students' capabilities and confidence in asking for feedback. Fourth-grade students in Jennifer Reed's classroom have self-assessed their performance using a single-point rubric (Figure 6.2). They rate themselves on the following scale:

1　I am just learning.

2　I am developing my understanding.

3　I understand and can teach others.

Figure 6.2　Self-Assessment of Writing

Rate 1, 2, or 3	Criteria for Success	Evidence
	I can hook the reader with an interesting beginning.	
	I can clearly state my opinion.	
	I can separate my reasons into paragraphs.	
	I can give evidence and examples to explain each of my reasons.	
	I can use transition words and phrases, like "for example," "for instance," "furthermore," and "in addition."	
	I can use high-level words to show I am an expert on my topic.	
	I can capitalize proper nouns and the beginnings of sentences.	

Rate 1, 2, or 3	Criteria for Success	Evidence
	I can put punctuation at the end of each sentence.	
	I can use commas to separate words in a series and before conjunctions.	
	In my conclusion I can write a concluding statement that reminds the reader of my opinion.	

online resources ↘ Available for download at **resources.corwin.com/teachingstudentstodrivetheirlearning**

Ms. Reed explains, "Today we have an opportunity to give and receive some peer feedback. Take some time to review your work and your rubric to prepare for those conversations." Fourth-grade students Sol and Jeremy sit next to each other and begin with Jeremy's opinion essay. Sol says, "I noticed that you have three reasons and you separated them into different paragraphs."

Jeremy looks up at the posted "Giving and Receiving Sentence Starters" (see Figure 6.3) and responds with, "Thank you for noticing that I thought of three reasons for why Nikola Telsa's inventions had more lasting impact than Alexander Graham Bell's." Jeremy continues, "I have my three reasons, but I don't think those paragraphs are long enough. I'm missing examples and details to back up my reasons. I think that's what I want your feedback about."

Figure 6.3   Giving and Receiving Sentence Starters

Giving	Receiving
I noticed that . . .	I appreciate you noticing that . . .
I wondered about . . .	I hadn't thought about that . . .
I was confused by . . .	I heard you say that . . . confused you.
I suggest that . . .	Based on your suggestion, I will . . .
Have you thought about . . .?	Thank you, what would you do?
You might consider . . .	I'm not sure what that looks like; tell me more.

CREATE FEEDBACK OPPORTUNITIES

An essential aspect of self-questioning and goal setting is in seeking feedback and help as needed. Interestingly, help seeking is not associated with helplessness but with empowerment and capacity building (Butler, 1998). In fact, avoiding help is associated with a host of negative learning outcomes, including lower achievement levels, unproductive "wheel spinning" (repeatedly getting something wrong), and poor ability to make accurate judgments about one's learning (Almeda et al., 2017). Help-seeking behaviors of students include asking for explanations to clarify understanding and seeking resources to support their learning. And help seeking has an effect size of 0.72, well worth our instructional attention.

But students don't always seek help or feedback from their teachers. Butler and Shibaz (2014) examined the function of positive student–teacher relationships in help seeking, noting that "whether students turn to a particular teacher depends crucially on whether they believe that the teacher cares about their students' welfare" (p. 50). This makes sense, of course. Any one of us is unlikely to seek help, no matter how much we may be aware of our own needs, from someone who does not appear to be all that caring.

In order for students to seek feedback, teachers need to create the conditions that allow this to flourish.

Help seeking is at the core of soliciting feedback and involves both the academic and social climate. Students who know how to drive their learning reliably and regularly seek feedback about their learning and progress toward goals. But in order for students to seek feedback, teachers need to create the conditions that can allow this to flourish. That means building and maintaining a strong and caring classroom learning climate, one in which students know they can approach teachers and classmates to get feedback.

One's willingness to seek feedback is influenced by prior knowledge. Students with higher levels of prior knowledge seek feedback about processes and understanding solutions, while those with lower prior knowledge seek low-level feedback about whether an answer is correct or not (Almeda et al., 2017). Sixth-grade math teacher Shekar Arya uses a variation of worked examples during small group math instruction to foster peer feedback. After he poses a problem, his students attempt to solve it independently. Mr. Arya examines each solution and then selects his "favorite no"—an incorrect answer containing some good mathematical thinking. "I give the incorrect solution back to the student and encourage them to confer with the other students to do two things. The first is to figure out where the error occurred, and the second is to determine why I selected it as my favorite no," he explained.

Mr. Arya enjoys listening to the feedback students give one another, especially how they offer explanations, ask clarifying questions, and speculate about the mathematical reasoning demonstrated. "As a teacher, I get two things out of it. First, I get to listen to the sophistication of their critical thinking. Second, I can coach them to get even better at peer feedback. I want them to pursue more than the correct answer. I want them to see the value in what they can offer one another."

PAUSE
AND
PONDER

Feedback is described in this module as "the most underutilized approach teachers have at their disposal." What are some of your areas of success and areas for growth in your use of feedback with students? What actions will you take to seek feedback from your students?

_____

_____

_____

_____

_____

_____

_____

_____

_____

_____

SEEING ERRORS AS OPPORTUNITIES
FOR LEARNING (AND CELEBRATING THOSE ERRORS)

Let's get real. No one likes to be wrong. When was the last time you failed at doing something and cheerily reminded yourself, "Now I've got an opportunity to learn!" The failure to accomplish something can be demoralizing and frustrating, especially in the absence of support. However, failure can also be productive, especially when it is followed with further instruction and feedback. Imagine what it would be like if classrooms were places where errors were celebrated as opportunities to learn. Over time, we might all learn to welcome the opportunities that our errors provide us for learning.

> Failure can also be productive, especially when it is followed with further instruction and feedback.

Kapur (2016) describes four possible learning events: *unproductive failure* (unguided problem solving), *unproductive success* (memorizing an algorithm without understanding why), *productive failure* (using prior knowledge to figure out a solution, followed by more instruction), and *productive success* (structured problem solving). Of the four conditions, unproductive failure yields the smallest gains, as students' thinking is not guided in any way, and they are just expected to discover what should be learned. Unproductive success is also of limited value, as students in this condition rely on memorization only but don't ever get to why and how this is applied. There's just no transfer of knowledge.

Now let's move to the beneficial conditions: productive failure and productive success. Kapur explains that

> the difference between productive failure and productive success is a subtle but an important one. The goal for productive failure is a preparation for learning from subsequent instruction. Thus, it does not matter if students do not

achieve successful problem-solving performance initially. In contrast, the goal for productive success is to learn through a successful problem-solving activity itself. (p. 293)

Both are necessary for learning. In productive success conditions, students are guided to resolve problems (not just memorize formulas). For instance, in a close reading lesson, students approach a complex text that stretches their deep comprehension, as the teacher carefully scaffolds their understanding by posing text-dependent questions that move from the literal to the structural to the inferential. But for students to drive their learning, they need to also experience productive failure. Keep in mind that these are opportunities for students to apply what they already know in an attempt to resolve a problem, with further subsequent supports available to refine their knowledge. These are small but important failures, not the soul-crushing kind that makes students want to throw up their hands in frustration. Figure 6.4 summarizes these types of learning events and their outcomes. To extend our close reading example, students sometimes take on complex texts initially in the company of peers, even if this effort is initially unsuccessful. After students have had a chance to use what they know, the teacher joins them to provide further instruction.

> For students to drive their learning, they also need to also experience productive failure.

Figure 6.4   Four Possible Learning Events

Type of Learning Event	Unproductive Failure	Unproductive Success	Productive Success	Productive Failure
	Unguided problem solving without further instruction	Rote memorization without conceptual understanding	Guided problem solving using prior knowledge and tasks planned for success	Unsuccessful or suboptimal problem solving using prior knowledge, followed by further instruction
Learning outcome	Frustration that leads to abandoning learning	Completion of the task without understanding its purpose or relevance	Consolidation of learning through scaffolded practice	Learning from errors; learners persist in generating and exploring representations and solutions
Useful for . . .			Surface learning of new knowledge firmly anchored to prior knowledge	Deep learning and transfer of knowledge
Undermines . . .	Agency and motivation	Goal setting and willingness to seek challenge		
Promotes . . .			Skill development and concept attainment	Use of cognitive, metacognitive, and affective strategies

↗ TEACHER ACTIONS

Consider the following actions that reinforce or derail efforts to ensure that students seek feedback and recognize that errors are opportunities to learn. We have included blank lines for you to add your ideas.

Teacher Actions That Reinforce Students' Ability to Seek Feedback and Recognize That Errors Are Opportunities to Learn	Teacher Actions That Derail Students' Ability to Seek Feedback and Recognize That Errors Are Opportunities to Learn
• Modeling seeking feedback and the excitement of using feedback to make improvements • Modeling making mistakes and learning something from the mistakes • Leveraging clear success criteria to support peer-to-peer feedback • Giving students the opportunity to use what they know before stepping in to refine knowledge or further develop skills	• Assuming that the feedback given was received • Waiting until the end of the assignment to provide feedback • Asking students to give peer-to-peer feedback without clear communication of the success criteria • Asking students to memorize information or complete tasks without understanding the relevance

CONCLUSION

Feedback and challenge can play a reciprocal role in fueling the learning of students. The feedback opportunities we create for students should correspond to three avenues: self, peers, and teachers. Consider it this way—in an environment where students are making errors, they need to be drenched in feedback to regain momentum, think strategically, and take action. In places where feedback is nonexistent or unproductive, learners can become paralyzed or even give up. Worst of all, they might rightly come to the conclusion that they're better off playing it safe because errors just make them feel sorry. As we noted in Module 1, challenge ("not too hard, not too boring") is a high-yield approach to learning. The students in Mr. Kearney's class aren't afraid of some challenge, in part because he has created the conditions that make the learning environment optimal for some academic risk taking. In the module that follows, we'll examine practices that he and other teachers like him utilize to ensure that students are equal participants in their own learning.

In an environment where students are making errors, they need to be drenched in feedback to regain momentum, think strategically, and take action.

NOTES

RETELLING PYRAMID

Create a pyramid of words, using the following prompts, that provides summarizing information. You're more likely to remember this information if you share with a peer.

1. One word that conveys an important topic in this module

2. Two words for an idea to support successful peer-to-peer feedback

3. Three words for actions you can take based on this module

4. Four words that are key to your understanding

5. Five words that convey a goal you have based on this module

_____

_____   _____

_____   _____   _____

_____   _____   _____   _____

_____   _____   _____   _____   _____

Revisit the Text Impression summary you developed at the beginning of this module, and compare it to your current level of understanding. Where did your learning deepen?

_____
_____
_____
_____
_____
_____
_____
_____
_____
_____
_____
_____
_____
_____

Using the traffic light scale, with red being not confident, yellow being somewhat confident, and green indicating very confident, how confident are you in your ability to

- Explain empathetic feedback?

- Describe the five aspects of the GREAT feedback framework?

- Identify the four types of feedback?

- Create feedback opportunities and model seeking feedback?

- Describe the learning outcomes of the four possible learning events?

LEARNERS RECOGNIZE THEIR LEARNING AND TEACH OTHERS

LEARNING INTENTION

We are learning to build learners' capacity to recognize their learning and teach others.

SUCCESS CRITERIA

- I can identify strategies for supporting student self-assessment and self-grading.

- I can implement strategies for retrieval practice.

- I can support students' metacognition through formative practice assessments.

- I can explore approaches for students to transfer learning through teaching others.

How does anyone know when they have learned something? It's hard to recognize the exact moment when learning has occurred, and more often than not, we realized that we have learned something long after the fact. Merriam-Webster defines learning as "gaining knowledge or understanding of or skill in by study, instruction, or experience." But that's not very actionable, and it's hard to recognize *when* learning occurs with this definition. Krupp (2007) suggested, "You've learned something if you can answer a question that you could not have answered previously." But is it really as simple as that? Is answering questions sufficient when it comes to learning?

Werft (2019) frames this differently, suggesting, "Whether you need to learn a new skill (action based), grow awareness or change attitudes (emotion based), or acquire new cognitive concepts (knowledge based)," start by asking yourself:

1. What new habits do I have to build during the learning process?

2. What level of knowledge do I need to demonstrate?

This model is much more actionable and notes that there are different types of learning. It also indicates that there are actions, both cognitive and metacognitive, that learners take to ensure that learning has occurred. Learning is complicated and complex. To generalize the evidence about learning, we'll use a simple three-phase model:

- Focus—intentional exposure to information in a variety of formats

- Store—transferring information from working memory to long-term memory

- Access—retrieving stored information from memory

These phases are important and are built into the learning experiences teachers design. We provide students with access to information through direct instruction, modeling, videos, lectures, and so on. But that's only part of the process, as students need to work with the information and transfer it from working to long-term memory. Again, there are several classroom structures that facilitate this transfer, including scaffolding and peer-to-peer interactions. We focused on several of these in Module 4 on selecting tools for learning, but many more are beyond the scope of this playbook.

> Students need to work with the information and transfer it from working to long-term memory.

It is worth noting that this model requires retrieval practice, which strongly impacts learning (Agarwal et al., 2021). In fact, based on their analysis of 50 experiments with over 5,000 students, these researchers note that "retrieval practice improved student learning to a greater extent than time spent on other classroom activities (e.g., reviewing material, lectures without quizzes)" (p. 1431).

TEXT IMPRESSION

Use the following words (in any order that works for you) to create an impression about what you think will be covered in this module.

retrieval practice • self-grading • think-alouds • teach-back • practice tests

_____

_____

_____

_____

_____

_____

_____

_____

_____

_____

_____

_____

Student self-assessments have been highlighted in a variety of forms throughout this book because the ability to self-assess is such a powerful engine for learning. It confirms for students what they have learned. Even better news is that teachers can equip students with tools to determine their own learning. Rubrics can also be used for students to self-assess. For instance, Anthony Escartín asks his middle school science students to examine their individual projects against a rubric, highlight the levels they believe they have attained, and then attach their self-assessment to the project. This practice can be quite useful for promoting self-assessment, helping students identify what they have learned so that they can teach others, and also recognizing future learning needs.

> Self-assessments can come in the form of a series of questions that prompt students to evaluate their learning.

Alternatively, self-assessments can come in the form of a series of questions that prompt students to evaluate their learning. High school business teacher James Cotton introduced quality assurance questions to his high school career and technical education students at the beginning of their first course. "We learned about the Deming process for quality assurance," explained Diana, one of the students in the program. "Plan, do, study, act." Pointing to a large poster on the wall, Diana read her teacher's quality assurance questions:

- **Plan:** Do I have a clear purpose and objectives?

- **Do:** Have I developed a sequence of steps to follow? Have I included testing points to see if this is meeting my objectives?

- **Study:** What are the possible causes of the problems I identify through testing?

- **Act:** Am I revising my plan and taking action until I am successful?

Diana explained that her team was developing a new yearbook product for sale at their school and that she is the project manager. She said,

> We developed a plan and set up steps, like surveying students about price points, print, and online features they wanted, and items they could do without. Then we had to meet with the yearbook staff to share our survey results. But then, there were some problems. They had all these questions—like we didn't break down the data, so we couldn't tell them about responses by grade level. So then we had to go into "study" mode. The yearbook staff was our test, and we didn't succeed.

Diana's team revised their plan, meeting with the yearbook editor and the adviser to determine what they needed to learn, and then redesigned the survey. "Today in class, we're looking at the numbers, and then we'll schedule another time to meet [with the yearbook editor]. That's our next step before we can go forward," said Diana.

"But here's the weird thing. I've just sort of figured out it works for lots of projects, not just here," she said. "I've got geometry homework tonight, and I'll be using the same process to get it done."

Confidence ratings are another means for students to self-assess.

Confidence ratings are another means for students to self-assess. Young children can use a "fist-to-five" method (anything from a closed hand to all five fingers displayed) to indicate their perceived success at the completion of a task, such as their knowledge level about something they have recently learned. Second-grade teacher Leona Simons introduced this method to her students at the beginning of the year. "I'd teach them some content and then do a check-in," she said. "Like we'd be learning about supply and demand in social studies, and I would ask them to hold a hand close to their chest so just I could see it. They would rank themselves from a fist [no understanding] to five fingers [very confident] about their ability to explain the difference between the two."

The teacher said that most of her students were doing it without prompting by the end of the first quarter. "Here's an example. I met with Kendrick this morning about his reading. He had selected a title that seemed a bit of a stretch for him. My face must have looked a little doubtful, because he said, 'It's a five for me, Ms. Simons. I already know a lot about taking care of dogs [the subject of the book]. My mom said we can get one after I learn more about caring for a dog. I think I can read it. But if it's too hard, I know what to do.'" The teacher smiled and shrugged. "How can I argue with that?" she said.

PAUSE
AND
PONDER

What benefits do you envision in your classroom if your students use self-assessment?

_____

_____

_____

_____

_____

_____

_____

_____

_____

What concerns do you have and how might you mitigate them?

_____

_____

_____

_____

_____

_____

_____

_____

_____

_____

_____

PEER GRADING AND SELF-GRADING

One common assessment practice in classrooms is having students grade each other's work. There are practical benefits to this in terms of time management, but there is also the idea that learning can occur through a carefully constructed peer evaluation process. Of course, this practice has confidentiality challenges and the potential for students to tease others who do not do well. Students must be taught how to provide growth-producing feedback (feedback literacy), and the classroom climate needs to be crafted so that errors are celebrated and not a source of shame.

Less common is self-grading, where students evaluate their own performance. But there can be great value in self-grading assignments and tasks, where the benefit is students' ability to recognize what has already been learned and what steps they need to take next to continue learning. Sadler and Good (2006) examined self-grading and peer grading in middle school classrooms. When peer grading, the identity of the learner was blinded so as not to socially influence the peer grader. Importantly, the students had been taught how to grade using rubrics—that's a critical point. Rubrics are of tremendous value when used properly—upfront at the beginning of the task—because well-constructed ones provide a clear map of the success criteria. They become all the more useful when further applied in peer and self-assessment. However, they are virtually useless when distributed for the first time just before the assessment. The teacher also independently graded their work, checking for accuracy and offering further feedback. The researchers discovered that the grades students awarded themselves and others were reasonably aligned with the teacher's evaluation, suggesting that these learners had a good grasp of the success criteria.

But on unannounced follow-up assessments, the students who graded their own work outperformed those who had been graded by peers. Why? The researchers specu-late that while the metacognitive benefits of peer and self-grading were both strong, the act of examining one's own work offered deeper insight and allowed the learners to make better decisions about their next steps. In the words of one seventh grader quoted in the study, "This felt strange at first . . . but by the end . . . I realized grading was another way of learning" (Sadler & Good, 2006, p. 25).

Fourth-grade student Ernesto is in a classroom that regularly employs self-grading. He explained that "the teacher still checks, so it's not like you can just give yourself a good grade," but he has noticed the benefits in his own learning. "We had math word problems last week, and we had to get the answer and explain the reasoning we used," he said. "But when I [graded] my own [paper], I had to give myself a 2 [on a 4-point rubric] for some of my answers, because I didn't always have some good math reasoning."

He showed one example. "See I had the right answer [pointing to the paper], but this problem was asking for me to prove it and use reasoning. I drew a model with little cubes to show how it could work, but it was for only the beginning of the problem. It wasn't all the way through. It was just where I started." When asked how this had impacted his thinking, he paused for a few moments and then said, "Well, I know I need to check to see if I can explain it through to the end of the problem, not just the place I start." Ernesto's teacher, Janine French, added, "When I graded his paper after he did, I saw the same omission he did. So I added feedback about the processes he was using to continue his thinking all the way through to the end of the problem."

 CONNECTIONS

How might you use this in your classroom?

Aspect of Learning	Definition	How I Might Use This . . .
Self-assessment		
Self-grading		

FORMATIVE PRACTICE TESTS

One way to implement retrieval practice is practice testing, which has an effect size of 0.46. Practice tests provide students with an opportunity to take short quizzes to understand their command of the subject or topic. These formative practice tests are low stake and not part of the student's grade, as the emphasis here is on practice to gain self-knowledge of learning gaps. A meta-analysis of the effectiveness of formative practice testing on advancing student learning reported these findings (Adesope et al., 2017):

- Lots of practice tests didn't increase student learning. One is often enough.

- Feedback paired with the practice test enhances learning.

- The usefulness of practice tests was strong at both the elementary and secondary levels.

- The value of formative practice tests is in students reflecting on their results.

Practice tests provide students an opportunity to take short quizzes to understand their command of the subject or topic.

Formative practice testing is not limited to paper-and-pencil or online quizzes. Classroom audience response systems are another form and have the added benefit of providing instant results. Sixth-grade English teacher Ivan Millan uses an audience response system that allows him to scan student responses on his tablet and display the results. His students have been reading *Among the Hidden* (Haddix, 2000), about an unnamed future society where food shortages and drought have led to a government decree that families cannot have more than two children. Luke, a third child, must be hidden away so that he will not be captured by the Population Police.

Mr. Millan poses comprehension questions for his students to respond to so that they can gauge their understanding of the book. After taking a five-question audience response quiz about three-quarters of the way through the novel, the students in his class analyzed their results and met in teams aligned to the questions. Ana did not answer two of the questions correctly but was especially puzzled by the fourth question, which asked about a historical allusion to American Revolutionary War patriot Patrick Henry's statement, "Give me liberty or give me death."

Ana met with a group of students who had selected the same question to build each other's knowledge. Ana and several other students searched for the quote online and read the background information about it. "Oh, I remember this now!" she said. "We learned about him [Patrick Henry] last year in social studies, right?" Ana and the others reaffirmed their background knowledge and tied Henry's act to the protest the children in the novel were planning. Ana later remarked, "When I read that Luke 'found it in an old book' it went right past me. I like the quizzes he [Mr. Millan] gives, because they help me see things I didn't notice the first time. I'm reading Chapters 23 and 24 tonight, so I'll look for things about being a patriot."

Figure 7.1 contains a tool that students can use to analyze their performance on practice tests. Note that they must complete the analysis, knowing the difference between complex items and more foundational items. Foundational items are generally those skills and concepts that are at the surface level, whereas complex items require deeper learning. Students also analyze their strengths and areas that they need to study or learn.

Figure 7.1 Analysis of Practice Test

Complex Items I Got Wrong	Complex Items I Got Right

Foundational Items I Got Wrong	Foundational Items I Got Right

What did I do well?	What can I teach others?	What do I need to practice?	What do I need someone to teach me?

online resources Available for download at **resources.corwin.com/teachingstudentstodrivetheirlearning**

INTERPRETING THEIR OWN DATA

Students own their own data, and as owners, students should be the consumers of their performance results, not just the teacher. However, in practice, that is not always the case, even with the advent of digital gradebooks, which make it much easier for students to see their own progress. Data about their progress toward goals not only assists students in making strategic decisions about current learning but can also signal to them when they are ready for the next challenge. Some of the simplest ways to do so are to have students keep physical or digital data logs that can display results in graph or chart form.

For example, we use graph paper for students to see what they have accomplished on timed writing events such as power writing (Fisher & Frey, 2007). Students write in three one-minute rounds to build writing fluency and then reread what they have written. Students are reminded to "write as much as you can, as well as you can" (Fearn & Farnan, 2001, p. 196). A word or phrase is posted on the board, and students are asked to use it somewhere in their writing. The timer is set, writing begins, and it continues until the timer rings a minute later. When time is up, students reread what they have written, circling any errors they notice, and then count and record in the margin the number of words they wrote. This routine is repeated two more times, until there are three one-minute writing samples in their journals. They record the highest number of words written (often it is the third sample) on a sheet of graph paper kept in their notebook. Thus, students can see their own progress over an extended period of time, as they become more fluent writers.

Students can track their progress on other skills and accomplishments. Some learning management systems and electronic gradebooks offer statistics on scores relative to the class. A student knowing, for example, that he scored in the lowest 20% of the class on the last science competency test provides more information to him than knowing that he got a grade of C. While the latter represents an average performance in terms of the criteria for the test, the former also provides information about his performance relative to the class. We are not advocating for grading on a curve or publicly displaying this information, but rather in signaling to the student that his perception of "average" may be limited, given that 80% of the class outperformed him. These class learning analytics are underutilized but offer potential for helping students understand their next steps. Students don't simply show up to class knowing how to assess their own learning. Their ability to do so is fostered by teachers who seek to build students' capacity to be "leaders of their own learning" (Berger et al., 2014).

----------------------•
Foundational items are generally those skills and concepts that are at the surface level, whereas complex items require deeper learning.

NOTES
_____

_____

_____

_____

_____

_____

_____

▱► NOTE TO SELF

Questions	Notes and Reflections
How have I used practice tests?	
What is my level of expertise (beginning, progressing, or consistent) in providing opportunities for students to use formative practice tests to recognize their learning?	
What are my next steps?	

OPPORTUNITIES TO TEACH OTHERS

Students who drive their learning are also driven to teach others what they have learned. There's a thrill that comes with providing another person with knowledge and skills, which is why so many of us became teachers. When we asked students how they know they have learned something, they did not focus on the answers we presented at the outset of this module. They consistently said some version of the same thing: "I know I have learned something when I can teach it to someone else." Imagine how different our classrooms, not to mention the world, would be if we all accepted this moral imperative: When you know something, you are responsible for teaching others.

> Students who drive their learning are also driven to teach others what they have learned.

The learning conditions in the classroom need to be set such that peer consultations can occur. Pausing lessons so that students can check in with one another can build the habit of conferring with others. These can range from partner checks ("take a moment and check with your partner to see if you both have the correct materials you'll need for this project") to more extended peer consultations. Our math colleague Joseph Assof uses a process called peer-assisted reflection (PAR; Reinholz, 2015) with his students. The premise of PAR is based on the differences between novices and mathematicians in approaching difficult problems. While novices hastily identify one tool and then use it exclusively until the bitter end of the calculations, mathematicians use iterative processes, including analyzing, exploring, planning, implementing, and verifying (Schoenfeld, 1992).

Students in Mr. Assof's classes complete one identified problem as a PAR problem, which requires that students write their reasoning as well as the calculations and solution. Students exchange the PAR problem with a partner the following day. Each partner examines the work the peer completed and provides feedback about processes or solutions. This process typically takes about ten minutes, at which point the students receive their original papers back, now annotated with new ideas. The teams then discuss the feedback, and both students make any corrections needed before submitting their papers to the teacher. "This is what we mean by mathematical thinking," explained Mr. Assof. "Students appreciate seeing how other classmates solved the same problem, sometimes using different processes. It gets them thinking about how they can think more flexibly and what benefit there is to talking with others."

TEACHING EACH OTHER WITH STUDENT THINK-ALOUDS

Teachers have used think-alouds for decades to model reading comprehension strategies for their students (Davey, 1983). The purpose of a think-aloud is to voice the internal cognitive and metacognitive decisions one makes while reading a passage. Fourth-grade teacher Isabelle Franklin uses a passage from the science textbook about the differing layers of a canyon's walls, which provide evidence of a geological record over millions of years. She thinks aloud about what she is reading, and how this triggers a decision on her part:

> So as I'm reading this paragraph, I'm getting the urge to put this down in my science journal. There are two things that are nudging me. The first is that I can see that this is an important concept. There are lots of clues, like the title of the passage and the photograph that supports it. The second thing that's nudging me is that there's lots of descriptive information here about the layers. I want a picture, but there isn't a diagram in the book. So I'm deciding to take

a pause here and draw a diagram of my own in my notebook. I don't need to be a great artist. But I do need to get the layers labeled in the correct order. I've learned from experience that when I take the time to draw something like this in my notebook, I remember the information better.

Ms. Franklin's think-aloud included why she was choosing to record her notes in this fashion. That is an item that we quite frankly often forget to share with students. Ms. Franklin creates opportunities for students to try on their own expert thinking as well, knowing that this is a mechanism for helping them become aware of their own learning, especially in the process of teaching another peer.

She uses student think-alouds (Baumann et al., 1993) to promote transfer about the learning decisions her students need to make. "It's more than plug n' chug," she reminds them. "Scholars like you know *why* you're doing something." Ms. Franklin keeps a checklist for student think-alouds posted in her classroom (see Figure 7.2). She posts a question for her students and asks them to think aloud with their partners as they consider what they know and why. "Are the top layers of a canyon's wall the youngest or the oldest? How do you know?" Bethany and Sam watch a 90-second video on the layers of the Grand Canyon a few times, and then Bethany begins:

> The narrator said that the sides of a canyon are like a book and that each of the layers is like a chapter in the book. He never said if the top of the rim was the youngest or the oldest. But he said something about the top layers being there before the ancient sea came in. Since he said "before" I think that means that they would be the youngest.

Sam continues:

> I think so, too. I was thinking about what we learned about how water cut through the rock layers. So the top would be the youngest and the bottom would be the oldest. It wasn't in the video, but it was something we read before. I'm thinking about that information when I'm listening to the video.

By modeling expert decision making and creating opportunities for students to explain their own learning, teachers give students a chance to become more adept and assured of their ability to choose strategies and become cognizant of their learning.

When teachers model expert decision making and create opportunities for students to explain their own learning, students become more adept and assured of their ability to choose strategies and become cognizant of their learning.

Figure 7.2   Student Think-Aloud Checklist

☐ Let your listener(s) read through the entire question or text before you begin your think-aloud.

☐ Use "I" statements.

☐ Explain why you think you are correct, or how you know you are.

☐ Speak loudly enough for your partner(s) to hear.

☐ Don't go too fast or too slow.

☐ Make sure your think-aloud doesn't go on for more than five minutes.

online resources ⟋ Available for download at **resources.corwin.com/teachingstudentstodrivetheirlearning**

TEACHING EACH OTHER WITH RECIPROCAL TEACHING

Reciprocal teaching (Palincsar & Brown, 1984) is a highly effective way to apply comprehension strategies throughout a text and has an effect size of 0.74. Students read collaboratively in small groups using text that has been segmented into passages of a few paragraphs each. At each stopping point, the group has a discussion about what they have just read, using four comprehension strategies:

- Summarizing the passage for key understandings

- Posing questions about the passage

- Clarifying unfamiliar vocabulary or concepts

- Predicting what the next passage will offer in terms of information

Once students have been taught the reciprocal teaching (RT) protocol (often estimated to take a few weeks), increased attention should be placed on the nature of the discourse itself, as students take on more control. Therefore, the role assignments that may be utilized when first learning the protocol (summarizer, questioner, clarifier, predictor) are faded as more natural discussions emerge. The true value of RT is that it affords all the members of the group a chance to teach one another, and in turn, be taught by peers.

The sixth-grade team at Mountain View Middle School spent the early weeks of the school year introducing and reinforcing RT in all of their classes. "This collaborative effort helped us spread the workload among all of us so that we could use it all year long," explained English teacher Arief Khouri. Once the students learned about the roles and procedures of RT, they were able to use it more flexibly. Social studies teacher Martin Andrews routinely uses it with primary source documents featured in the textbook. "We're studying ancient history, and these documents are pretty archaic. They're a lot harder to understand than the rest of the textbook," said Mr. Andrews. "To tell the truth, I used to skip these, because when I assigned them, the kids didn't understand them. Using the RT protocol has given me a tool to assist with that." Mr. Khouri added, "What's got me stoked is that I hear my students having conversations like RT even when we're not specifically doing [the protocol]. That's proof for me that this has become a transfer skill, not just something the teacher makes you do."

> When students share their learning with others in the class, peers profit from witnessing explanations that are coming from someone who is learning alongside them.

TEACHING EACH OTHER WITH PEER TEACHING AND TUTORING

In addition to the emotional support that peers can learn to provide, peer tutoring is an effective approach that develops transfer of learning, by which we mean that students can use the concepts and skills flexibly and in new situations. Peer tutoring has an effect size of 0.54 on the one receiving the tutoring, and an effect size of 0.48 on the one doing the tutoring. In other words, it's good for both those giving and receiving tutoring. Figure 7.3 contains a list of different peer-tutoring models.

Figure 7.3   Models of Peer Tutoring

- **Classwide Peer Tutoring (CWPT):** At specific times each week, the class is divided into groups of two to five students. The goal is to practice or review skills and content, rather than introduce new learning. Each student in the group has an opportunity to be both the tutee and the tutor. The teacher typically assigns the content to be covered during these sessions, which includes a peer explaining the work, asking questions of the group, and providing feedback to the peer(s). CWPT involves structured procedures and direct rehearsal, and it may include competitive teams with the scores posted (Maheady et al., 2001).

- **Cross-Age Peer Tutoring:** Older students are paired with younger students, and the older students have the responsibility to serve as tutor. The roles do not change, but the current performance levels of the tutor and tutee may be similar. The tutors explain concepts, model appropriate behavior, ask questions, and encourage better study habits. Tutors may even be taught to design lessons for their younger students (e.g., Jacobson et al., 2001).

- **Peer-Assisted Learning Strategies (PALS):** Pairs of students work together, taking turns tutoring and being tutored. Teachers train students to use the following learning strategies for reading: passage reading with partners, paragraph "shrinking" (or describing the main idea), and prediction relay (predicting what is likely to happen next in the passage) (L. S. Fuchs et al., 1999; D. Fuchs et al., 2000).

- **Same-Age Peer Tutoring:** Like classwide peer tutoring, there are opportunities to create tutoring structures across a grade level or content area (Moliner & Alegre, 2020). In some cases, the same-age peers are within the same classroom, and other times they collaborate across classrooms. In same-age tutoring, not all the students are engaged in tutoring at the same time, as would be the case for CWPT. Again, the teacher trains the tutors on their role and establishes routines for the same-age tutoring.

- **Reciprocal Peer Tutoring (RPT):** In this format of peer tutoring, students are paired at random to support the learning of their peers. It's essentially a collaborative learning task that involves students with similar academic backgrounds working together. Each partnership is responsible for synthesizing content, preparing tasks, asking questions, and providing answers to their questions and explanations for their answers. Often students develop practice tests during RPT and then identify areas of additional learning needed (e.g., Alegre-Ansuategui et al., 2017).

Source: Frey et al. (2023).

In Natasha Walker's kindergarten class, she provides opportunities for learners to work with their "sound partners" at least three times per week. Yesterday a new sound was introduced, and today students are using their "what sound?" protocol to provide corrective feedback to each other. Each student has the opportunity to be both coach and reader.

Joshua and Martita are both sitting on the carpet with a laminated card in front of them (Figure 7.4). Joshua's role is to be the coach, so he points to a letter and asks, "What sound?" When Martita produces the correct phoneme to match the letter, he says, "Good job." If she gets stuck or says an incorrect sound he says, "Pause. This sound is ___. What sound?" Then he has her try the line again.

After Martita successfully finishes producing the sounds, Martita smiles and says, "Now it's my turn to be coach!"

Ms. Walker explains, "This is an excellent opportunity for children to have more practice with the sounds and letters we are practicing. They are motivated by the ability to get their turn as the coach, but I appreciate the multiple chances for feedback from their peers." Ms. Walker notes another benefit to this practice is that she can easily differentiate by individualizing the reading charts for each student or for each partnership. Structured activities like this one allow for multiple exposures to important reading skills, but they also build a community culture that values the growing expertise of students and their ability to support each other.

Figure 7.4   What Sound? Chart for Peer Tutoring

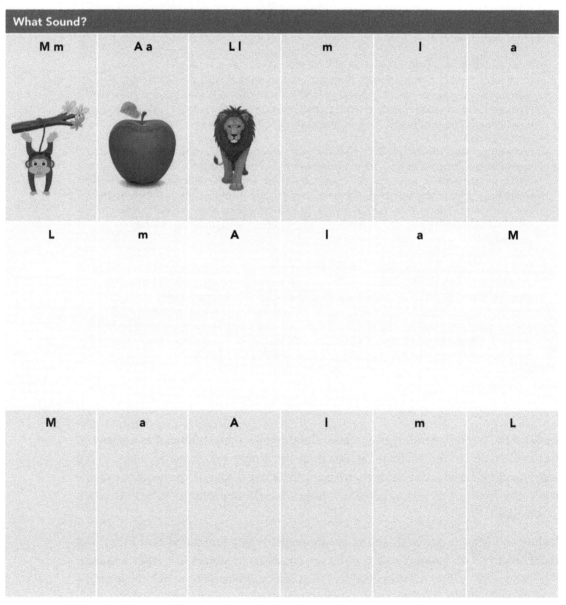

Image sources: Monkey: iStockphoto.com/blueringmedia; Apple: iStockphoto.com/Vectorigdit; Lion: iStockphoto.com/bounward

TEACHING EACH OTHER WITH TEACH-BACK

Students need opportunities to explain to others. When learning is shared with others in the class, peers profit from witnessing explanations that are coming from someone who is learning alongside them. Once a child has learned something, teaching it to someone else can assist in transfer or ownership of that learning. First discussed as an approach to increase patients' adherence to medical advice (e.g., Ha Dinh et al., 2016), teach-back has been used to solidify preK–12 students' learning as they reframe their learning and teach others (Fisher, Frey, Bustamante, & Hattie, 2021). These short, student-developed lessons allow learners to construct their knowledge by teaching something they are learning.

In teach-back, a student is assigned a skill or concept the class has been learning. Their challenge is to record themselves teaching it to others in one to two minutes. Young children, for example, might teach a sibling about a math skill they are learning. Older students might summarize important points to keep in mind to avoid plagiarism, calculate the area of a triangle, or assemble a dissection kit.

Fourth grader Jazmine created a Flipgrid lesson on comparisons of six-digit numbers. She has been learning about place values. Jazmine uses a whiteboard to demonstrate how she determines which of two numbers is larger. She moves through each place value until she arrives at the difference at the 10,000 place value. She asserts, "5 and 3 are not equal," and then explains how she uses the < sign (she calls it an alligator) in her mathematical equation.

CONCLUSION

The takeaway from this module is that students need to recognize their own learning and teach one another. Of course, students must be taught with intention about how to do so, and they must learn what to do with the information they provide and receive. In essence, students who drive their learning are really cultivating dispositions about being reflective and self-aware. They come to understand that their learning is a journey: there are no bad places to be, and they have the agency to move forward.

> Students who drive their learning . . . come to understand that their learning is a journey: there are no bad places to be, and they have the agency to move forward.

To develop this kind of thinking, teachers must ensure that their students do not rely exclusively on adults for information about needed areas of additional learning or improvement. Rather, students start to rely on themselves and know how to self-assess, rather than waiting passively for their teacher to tell them when they've learned something. In other words, they're active. They want to know their status so that they can improve even further. None of this is going to be accomplished if the tasks teachers assign are simple or lack complexity. Rich, rigorous tasks allow students an opportunity to struggle, to figure out what they still need to learn and when they are ready to move forward. This happens when their learning is visible and when they recognize that there are endless opportunities to learn.

 TEACHER ACTIONS

Consider the following actions that reinforce or derail efforts to ensure that students know what they have learned and have opportunities to teach others. We have included blank lines for you to add your ideas.

Teacher Actions That Reinforce Students' Knowing What They Learned and Teaching Others	Teacher Actions That Derail Students' Knowing What They Learned and Teaching Others
• Providing instruction on how to give growth-producing feedback • Planning opportunities for students to interpret the data and information gained from examining formative practice assessments • Placing value on the act of examining one's own work over correctness • Allowing students to hear the internal decision-making process of teachers • Fostering a culture of supportive peer relationships • Making intentional decisions about how to partner students	• Expecting students to use a rubric to self-assess with criteria that haven't been modeled or processed • Providing opportunities for peers to give each other feedback without training students in how to give feedback • Setting up peer-tutoring experiences without students having solidified their own skills • Setting up peer-tutoring experiences with some students never getting the opportunity to be the tutor
_____	_____
_____	_____
_____	_____
_____	_____
_____	_____
_____	_____
_____	_____
_____	_____
_____	_____
_____	_____
_____	_____
_____	_____
_____	_____
_____	_____
_____	_____

RETELLING PYRAMID

Create a pyramid of words, using the following prompts, that provides summarizing information. You're more likely to remember this information if you share with a peer.

1. One word that conveys an important topic in this module

2. Two words for a type of peer-tutoring opportunity you would like to learn more about

3. Three words for actions you can take based on this module

4. Four words that are key to your understanding

5. Five words that convey a goal you have based on this module

_____

_____   _____

_____   _____   _____

_____   _____   _____   _____

_____   _____   _____   _____   _____

Revisit the Text Impression summary you developed at the beginning of this module, and compare it to your current level of understanding. Where did your learning deepen?

_____

_____

_____

_____

_____

_____

_____

_____

_____

_____

_____

_____

_____

_____

Using the traffic light scale, with red being not confident, yellow being somewhat confident, and green indicating very confident, how confident are you in your ability to

- Identify strategies for supporting student self-assessment and self-grading?

- Implement strategies for retrieval practice?

- Support students' metacognition through formative practice assessments?

- Explore approaches for students to transfer learning through teaching others?

8

RESPONDING WHEN STUDENTS DISENGAGE

LEARNING INTENTION

We are learning to recognize and respond when students disengage.

SUCCESS CRITERIA

- I can recognize signs of disrupting, withdrawing, and avoiding learning.
- I can describe nine cognitive barriers to learning.
- I can identify actions to take when cognitive barriers arise.

We have focused significant time and attention on teaching students to drive their learning. We have proposed six factors that are important if this learning is going to take hold. And we have argued that addressing these factors will increase the likelihood of engaging students in their learning. In doing so, we have focused on the right side of the engagement continuum in an effort to move students from the low bar of participating, to actually investing and driving their learning.

However, there is the other side of the engagement continuum—*disengagement*.

The left side plagues all of us as teachers. And it doesn't even have to be major disruptive events. The constant withdrawal and avoidance of learning behaviors are like 1,000 paper cuts that teachers seem to think that they must endure. Thankfully, there is evidence about why learners disengage and what we can do about it.

Before we explore the cognitive barriers to learning, we want to recognize that some students need significantly more support than others to move from the left side of the engagement continuum. However, take it as a win each and every time a student moves the next position to the right. To remind you, we've placed the continuum here again (see Figure 8.1).

> There is valuable evidence about why learners disengage and what we can do about it.

Figure 8.1   A Continuum of Engagement

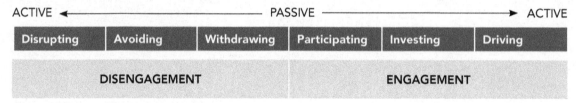

Source: Adapted from the work of Berry (2020).

As educator Noah Blake likes to say,

> If I can get the student to stop being disruptive and just avoid learning, it's progress. And then other students are not being distracted so I feel better. I have tools to interrupt the disruptions and a supportive admin team. I've also learned not to take it personally but then do my best to make the changes.

In fact, classroom management has an effect size of 0.35, just below average in terms of the impact on learning. Again, there are programs and systems to address students with significant behavioral issues that are beyond the scope of this playbook. This module focuses on the cognitive barriers to learning, which often force learners into avoiding and withdrawing from learning.

TEXT IMPRESSION

Use the following words (in any order that works for you) to create an impression about what you think will be covered in this module.

cognitive barriers • mental mindset • relevance • self-regulation • student mistrust • misconceptions • disengagement • cognitive load theory

_____

_____

_____

_____

_____

_____

_____

_____

_____

_____

_____

_____

COGNITIVE BARRIERS TO LEARNING

Jayden is sitting at a desk, apparently doing nothing related to school. When asked about what the class is learning, Jayden doesn't know. Jayden is not distracting anyone else, but clearly he isn't learning anything new. In too many classrooms, Jayden would be left alone. After all, he's just sitting quietly, so it's easy to overlook him. He has mastered the art of hiding in plain sight. With some silent students, it's seen as a blessing, because provoking the student may cause problematic behaviors, or so the common wisdom goes.

In another classroom, Jayden would be given a zero for participation or task completion and eventually would not pass the class. Or perhaps Jayden would be sent out of the room for discipline, especially if the behavior did not change when a change was requested by the teacher. We understand the rationale for each of these actions because it's frustrating not knowing what to do when students are avoiding or withdrawing from learning. But none of these responses resulted in a learning change for Jayden.

Our question—in fact, our quest—was deceptively simple. We wanted to know how educators respond when students are actively or passively disengaged. Our search led us to a review of studies by Chew and Cerbin (2021). Drawing on the evidence about how people learn, they proposed a framework for understanding nine cognitive challenges that interfere with learning and can cause learners to disengage. Further, they aligned this framework with research on how to troubleshoot these cognitive barriers. When we read these, we realized that we had encountered most of them personally in our teaching careers. In other words, these cognitive challenges to learning were not limited to school-aged students and apply to all of us. These barriers seemed universal in their ability to interfere with engagement and learning.

Here's the essential part of their review of the research on responses to disengagement. They note that there are actions teachers can take to re-engage students in order to address the challenges. The researchers state, "Teachers must determine the effective ways to resolve each challenge, but that solution may vary for different topics and students. Failure to navigate any of the challenges can undermine optimal learning" (Chew & Cerbin, 2021, pp. 3–4). We'll put a finer point on it: One size does not fit all. It is time we move beyond the myopic view that disengagement is strictly behavioral—time to understand disengagement cognitively and emotionally, to teach proactively to reduce disengagement, and to respond with precision when disengagement emerges.

PAUSE AND PONDER

We haven't introduced the cognitive barriers to learning yet, but what barriers come to mind based on what you just read? Remember that these are cognitive barriers—things happening in the minds of our learners.

_____

_____

_____

_____

_____

_____

_____

What barriers might Jayden have faced that caused learning to be compromised?

_____

_____

_____

_____

_____

_____

_____

_____

1. Mental Mindset

Sometimes, learners approach tasks as if they have no chance of success. They believe that they do not have the skills to accomplish the work in front of them. This compromised self-efficacy is rooted in a belief system that is likely inaccurate. As a result, learners barely put forth effort and often stop working on the task at hand. But mindset is not limited to individual tasks and can cover entire content areas. For example, there are students who believe that they will fail at mathematics, writing, reading, art, or whatever even before their first lesson. We had one student tell us that "math hates me" and that "nothing could be done to pass the class." That was the first day of ninth grade.

In this case, the teacher had to determine the student's current level of performance and then design experiences that allowed the student to experience success. The teacher also talked with the student about the impact of a fixed mindset when it came to math and how the student decided that learning would not occur before even meeting the teacher. The teacher said, "I'm pretty good at explaining the math and then having you practice until you learn. Did you notice that you're learning it? We need to trust the process and believe that we can do hard things."

Mental mindset also comes into play when learners do not find the task or learning relevant. If they believe that there is no reason to learn this stuff, they will likely disengage and focus their attention elsewhere. In this case, it's not self-efficacy but rather the belief that the content will not serve them well. When any of us fail to see the relevance in the content, we naturally devote our resources elsewhere.

Recall from Module 3 that educators can create relevance with students through *personal association, personal usefulness,* or *personal identification.* Our job description should include "make content interesting." Teachers need to explain why learning is worth the time and attention of students. When this does not occur, some students become compliant anyway, because they (or their parents) want grades, and others disengage from lessons and suffer the consequences of not learning.

CONNECTIONS

What mindsets might your students have that interfere with their learning?

_____

_____

_____

_____

_____

_____

(Continued)

(Continued)

How might you respond to these mindsets?

_____

_____

_____

_____

_____

_____

2. Metacognition and Self-Regulation

Some students disengage because they have not yet developed metacognitive self-regulation skills, which include understanding and managing behavior and reactions to feelings about the things happening. When learners do not act in their best interest, they exhibit a range of challenging behaviors, including lack of interest in school. Generally speaking, self-regulation skills include goal setting, self-monitoring, effective use of self-talk, and self-reinforcement. As noted, self-regulation is a skill that can be learned and "involves the modulation of one's thoughts, emotions, and behaviors in the pursuit of long-term goals" (Elhusseini et al., 2022). In fact, El Husseini and colleagues' systematic review of 46 studies on self-regulation interventions found that students across grade levels benefited on academic measures of reading, writing, and mathematics.

Much of this playbook has focused on developing self-regulation skills, including learning to drive learning. Teachers can integrate opportunities for students to plan, monitor, and adjust their learning in the lessons they create. We have focused on the importance of students having learning goals (we called them learning intentions and success criteria) and tools to monitor their own progress. We have also focused on seeking feedback and noticing when something has been learned. In other words, building cognitive self-regulation skills is deeply embedded into the experiences students have when teachers focus on students driving their learning. When students do not build these skills, they are much more likely to disengage.

Teachers need to explain to the class why learning is worth the students' time and attention.

We don't want to discount the fact that other students may already possess deep knowledge of a topic. Teachers can use the "must-do/may-do" model, in which students complete tasks from the must-do column, often in the order they want, and then work on extension activities from the may-do column until time is up. Of course, there is always the opportunity to teach others, but there are many more options that provide students with opportunities to extend what they have learned. Figure 8.2 includes a sample extension menu for elementary students.

Figure 8.2   Extension Menu for Elementary Students

Illustrate or draw (sketch to stretch).	Compose: Creative writing	Compare: What is alike or different?
Write an analogy or a mnemonic to help classmates understand or remember information.	Student choice	Create a board game.
Read all about it: What are two questions you still have about the text? How can you investigate your questions?	Create a survey. Poll classmates and create a graph to represent data.	Multiple perspectives: Convey two perspectives on the topic.

In some cases, learners are overconfident about what they know and can do. In these situations, students are likely to disengage, because they do not believe that the content is of use to them, because they have already learned it. When that is the case, teachers need to design learning experiences that allow students to self-assess their learning. Initial assessments in advance of instruction can highlight misconceptions or partial understandings held by the overconfident student.

Teachers can also confer with students, asking for explanations and justifications for their thinking. In a lesson about the causes of World War II, Kolby was tapping other students, flipping a pencil over and over, and asking to leave for the restroom and to get water. To address this behavior, Kolby's teacher gave the class a collaborative task so that the teacher and student could have a quick conversation about the lesson while the other students worked together. This resulted in the teacher understanding that Kolby believed that the United States entered World War II to free people from concentration camps. As Kolby said, "I already know all of this. I've seen like ten movies about World War II." In response, the teacher said, "What role did Pearl Harbor play in this?" Kolby responded, "I saw a movie about that, but that was after the war started." The teacher responded, "Could I ask you to make a quick timeline so that we can revisit the events leading up to the war? If you are willing, we could share the timeline with the class as a review." Kolby responded yes, and in making the timeline, realized that there was still much learning to do.

> In some cases, learners are overconfident about what they know and can do.

CONNECTIONS

Given the age group of students you teach, what can you do to extend their self-regulation?

_____

_____

_____

_____

_____

_____

_____

_____

How might you engage students who have already learned the content or finished their tasks?

_____

_____

_____

_____

_____

_____

_____

_____

_____

How might you respond when students are overconfident about their learning?

_____

_____

_____

_____

_____

_____

_____

_____

3. Student Fear and Mistrust

When any of us are living in a state of fear or mistrust, learning is harder, and we probably will disengage from the tasks assigned to us. When students are being bullied, fear increases and learning decreases. In fact, the effect size for bullying is −0.33, a very negative significant impact on the learning of students who experience emotional and physical abuse from their peers. When students have experienced abuse and live in a state of fear, they learn less. The effect size for maltreated children is −0.63. It's hard to learn when people hurt you. And when students believe that the teacher or their peers dislike them, the impact on learning is also significant, with an effect size of −0.26.

In the world of language acquisition, the affective filter theory suggests that anxiety blocks learning. The effect size of anxiety is −0.36, which indicates that this emotional state interferes with learning. The key to addressing this is to teach students coping strategies that they can use. Of course, if students are abused, or if they suffer from bullying, additional resources are necessary, and school leadership needs to be involved. In addition, teachers can focus on their credibility with students, building trust so students recognize that teachers have their best interests at heart and that they are safe in the classroom. The climate of the classroom is critical, and it needs to be one in which mistakes are recognized as opportunities to learn, rather than reasons for shame and humiliation.

> When students are being bullied, their fear increases and their learning decreases.

Interestingly, there is evidence that some students see feedback as a sign that the teacher does not like them (e.g., Taggart & Laughlin, 2017). The teacher is likely attempting to provide growth-producing feedback, but the student interprets it as further evidence that they are not liked. One way to address this is to ensure that feedback is asked for. Additionally, teachers can talk with students, building trust and working together to improve the learning so that students do not interpret feedback as a negative.

Additionally, teachers can build feedback literacy in students by helping them to understand the difference between feedback and criticism. Educator Deb Hanson suggests teaching students how to receive feedback, noting that much of it can ride on how a person interprets the feedback offered, whether from the teacher or peers (see Figure 8.3).

Figure 8.3 Criticism Versus Feedback

Fixed Mindset	Growth Mindset
This person is picking on me.	This person cares about me and is trying to help me.
This person thinks I'm bad at this.	This person must believe in me, or they wouldn't bother pointing out how I can improve.
I'm so angry. I feel so embarrassed.	I'm thankful this person is telling me how I can do this better.
I give up. I'll never be able to do this as well as this person wants me to.	I'll try to do the things this person suggests and see if it helps me improve.

Source: Hanson (2017).

PAUSE
AND
PONDER

How can you build trust with students?

_____

_____

_____

_____

_____

_____

_____

_____

_____

How might you structure feedback to ensure that students perceive it to be growth producing?

_____

_____

_____

_____

_____

_____

_____

_____

_____

_____

_____

4. Insufficient Prior Knowledge

When learners do not have sufficient prior knowledge for the new learning to make sense, they are likely to disengage. In essence, we go from the known to the new, and prior achievement plays a significant role in learning with an effect size of 0.82. The reality is that all of us have unfinished learning, and it gets in the way of our new learning. The challenge is that when too much attention is paid to the unfinished learning, deficit thinking starts to creep in. Instead, we need to take a strengths-based approach, which changes the focus to

Another valuable effort is to build feedback literacy in students by helping them to understand the difference between feedback and criticism.

- What a student can already do

- What a student can do when provided with educational support

- What a student will one day be able to do

Of course, there are actions that teachers can take to address unfinished learning. But, as we noted in Module 2, it starts with knowing what students already know. From there, teachers can identify critical knowledge and skills that students must learn. Remember, not everything from previous years is critical. As our colleague John Almarode reminds us, there is a difference between things that students **need** to know and things that would be **neat** to know.

When critical prior knowledge is missing, teachers can provide lessons in background knowledge. They can have students read, because reading widely in texts you can read is a very effective way to build background knowledge. They can also create short interactive videos that provide students with access to concepts (and terminology for those concepts). Interactive videos have an effect size of 0.54, probably because students actually have to respond to the content they are viewing—interactive videos are a much less passive experience than reading. For example, the students in Carla Bacerra's class were focused on inertia, and she wanted to ensure that students had sufficient background knowledge for their classroom experiment to make sense. Ms. Bacerra found a video online and added it to her learning management system, adding questions every minute or so. The system stopped the video at these insertions and popped up the questions, and it would not continue to play until students responded. Ms. Bacerra allows students to rewatch the videos if they respond incorrectly, as she believes that reviewing the videos will help address any unfinished learning. In essence, Ms. Bacerra knows that frequent, low-stakes assessments improve learning and encourage students to complete their review tasks (e.g., Sotola & Crede, 2021).

CONNECTIONS

What tools do you have to build background and address unfinished learning?

_____

_____

_____

_____

_____

_____

_____

_____

_____

(Continued)

(Continued)

What changes need to occur to adopt a strengths-based approach at your school?

_____

_____

_____

_____

_____

_____

_____

_____

_____

5. Misconceptions

Sometimes learners have misconceptions that interfere with their learning. Misconceptions are beliefs that are contradicted by the current evidence. For example, if a student believes that human growth is caused by cells getting larger, lessons about cellular structure and cellular division will likely be interpreted through the lens that they will get bigger in the process. This is a cognitive barrier to learning that prevents full understanding of the content.

When learners do not have sufficient prior knowledge for the new learning to make sense, they are likely to disengage.

Perhaps we will address a misconception you have. Teachers should start with the facts. When they start with the misconception, learners who hold that misconception will stop listening once their view is presented (Kowalski & Taylor, 2017). In fact, beginning with the misconception can trigger the "familiarity backfire effect," in which the belief in the misconception is strengthened (Cook & Lewandowsky, 2011). However, we recognize that it is popular to address student misconceptions at the outset of a lesson. The idea is that we need to take care of the misconception so that students can focus on the new learning. But the evidence suggests that this approach is backward. Did you notice that we presented the evidence first and then named the misconception? Hopefully, that allowed you to think about what you think and revise your conception of the world.

Addressing misconceptions requires that educators identify misconceptions. As teachers gain experience in a given content area with a group of students of a given age, they become increasingly astute with respect to common misconceptions. In addition, there are several tools that are useful in uncovering misconceptions, such as an anticipation guide (Duffelmeyer, 1994) in which several statements are presented to students, and they decide which are true and which are false. For example, middle school students in Faith Mack's class were focused on tracing the origins of Islam. As part of their studies, they watched a PBS video, and their teacher provided them with an anticipation guide to identify misconceptions and misunderstandings (see Figure 8.4).

> Sometimes learners have misconceptions that interfere with their learning.

Figure 8.4   Anticipation Guide for Islam Unit

Name: _____ Date: _____

Anticipation Guide for "Islam: Empire of Faith"

Directions: Read each statement and write a "+" for true statements and a "–" for false statements.

Statement	Before Viewing	After Viewing
Baghdad is the holy city of the Muslim faith.		
The Middle East is a natural land bridge between east and west.		
Merchants were the most influential people in Baghdad.		
Arabic numerals are still in use today.		
The growth of the Middle East can be traced to the Renaissance in Europe.		
Muslim scholars used the scientific process first described by the ancient Greeks.		
Muslim physicians invented hospitals.		
The development of the science of optics first began in the Islamic world.		
Discoveries about optics led to the later invention of the camera.		
Paper was first used in Egypt.		

To fully understand learner misconceptions, teachers can ask students to justify their thinking, either orally or in writing. In listening to or reading student responses, teachers can identify patterns in the class that need to be addressed. Again, we all have misconceptions, and they interfere with our learning. Addressing misconceptions with factual information can re-engage students in the learning and help them develop different conceptions about the world.

CONNECTIONS

What are the common misconceptions in your grade level or content area?

_____

_____

_____

_____

_____

_____

_____

_____

How might you unearth student misconceptions?

_____

_____

_____

_____

_____

_____

_____

_____

How did you respond to the "facts-first" approach to addressing misconceptions?

_____

_____

_____

_____

_____

_____

_____

_____

6. Ineffective Learning Strategies

Sometimes students have learning strategies, but they aren't working. When the student realizes this, they give up. Recognizing this cause of disengagement is fairly simple: The student got to work and then stopped. If that is the case, it may very well be that the learning tools are not working, and frustration has set in. Frustration has a negative impact on learning with an effect size of −0.52. As we have noted before, appropriate levels of challenge have a positive impact on learning, but if the student moves into frustration, the impact becomes negative.

One of the indicators that students can drive their learning is that they know what to do when they don't know what to do. If they do not know this, they are very likely to disengage. In part, the solution is to ensure that students are taught a range of learning tools and provided opportunities to select from those tools. It's also important to ensure that students know that they can give up on a learning strategy and try something else. Of course, using learning tools one time and then changing them is not likely to develop a habit. Much like learning content, students need spaced practice with learning tools for them to stick. The effect size of using spaced practice over massed practice is 0.65.

Study skills, as we noted in Module 4, help students develop a range of tools that they can use. In addition, teachers can model effective strategies with their think-alouds. Sometimes, students need to experience the ways in which others use learning tools and the decisions that others make about selecting those tools. Importantly, teacher modeling should include the how and why of selecting tools for learning. Simply providing students with examples of the thinking is not likely to ensure the adoption of those tools. In other words, there is a difference between "I can make the following prediction . . . " and "I can make the following prediction [x] because the author told me [y]." In the former, students know that their teacher can make predictions and what the predictions are. In the latter, they are apprenticed into the reasoning about how the prediction was made. The latter increases the likelihood that students will use the cognitive and metacognitive tools that are modeled for them.

> Sometimes students have learning strategies, but those approaches aren't working.

PAUSE AND PONDER

What tools do your students need to learn and practice?

_____

_____

_____

_____

_____

_____

_____

_____

_____

_____

(Continued)

(Continued)

How might you integrate study skills into your classroom practice?

_____

_____

_____

_____

_____

_____

_____

_____

_____

_____

_____

7. Transfer of Learning

Perhaps one of the most challenging cognitive challenges is the transfer of learning. Teaching to the point of transfer is difficult, especially if the climate and culture of the school favor surface learning. Transfer requires that students overpractice and overlearn to the point that they generalize and apply what they have learned in new situations and without the guidance of the teacher.

Teacher modeling
should include the how
and why of selecting
tools for learning.

When tasks require the application of previous learning and students have not reached the point of being able to apply what they have learned at the surface level, they are likely to disengage, as the tasks are not within their reach. However, teaching the same concepts and skills again will not suddenly engage the students, because they already have these abilities but don't know how to use them.

When students learn new skills and concepts, teachers need to plan tasks requiring near and far transfer. *Near transfer* occurs when the novel situation is paired closely with a learned situation. For example, a young child who is learning sight words has been able to recognize these words in isolation on flashcards but now can identify specific words in running text. The size of the leap is larger in *far transfer,* as the learner must be able to make connections between more seemingly remote situations. For example, when a student is able to consistently and correctly use the sight word *where* (not *were*) in her original writing, she has moved to far transfer.

Teachers can model how to use skills and concepts in different contexts, which provides students with examples of the thinking that they will need to do. When modeling is limited to the task at hand, students may develop a surface-level understanding but not know how to use that information later. In addition, teachers can tailor their feedback to include how students process the tasks. The process level of feedback

- Provides connections between ideas

- Employs task strategies for identifying errors

- Provides cues about different strategies

In providing this kind of feedback, teachers can help students develop strategies that allow them to apply, generalize, and transfer their learning to different situations.

When students are learning new skills and concepts, teachers need to plan tasks that require near transfer and far transfer.

PAUSE AND PONDER

How can you plan tasks that require near and far transfer?

_____

_____

_____

_____

_____

_____

_____

_____

_____

_____

How can you integrate process feedback into your practice?

_____

_____

_____

_____

_____

_____

_____

_____

_____

_____

_____

8. Constraints of Selective Attention

The myth of multitasking. We all think that we are the one human who can multitask despite decades worth of evidence that our brains do not do this (e.g., Crenshaw, 2008). It is true that we can engage in multiple motor behaviors at the same time, the proverbial walking and chewing gum. However, we cannot engage in multiple cognitive tasks at the same time. Some people can more rapidly shift between tasks than others, but we don't have dual-processing brains that allow for multiple cognitive tasks to be completed simultaneously. This is probably why the presence of mobile phones in school has a negative impact on learning, with an effect size of −0.34. Having said that, when phones are used as learning tools, the harm is reduced. The problem is that they are not used as learning tools because students generally believe that they can multitask, using their phones and attending to class at the same time.

In part, teachers need to model concentration, focus, and stamina for students. When the adults around them look like they are multitasking, students think they can do the same. We should talk with students about the myth of multitasking and the value of focusing on complex cognitive tasks while avoiding distractions. Some evidence also suggests that scheduled technology breaks can help students decide to engage, because they know that they will have time to update and check their technology at a specific time (e.g., Barshay, 2011). In essence, students check their technology because they fear missing out, they are bored, or because they believe that they can accomplish multiple cognitive tasks at the same time.

Whether technology is the cause of multitasking or something else is, such as trying to do assignments for one class in another class, teachers who have strong reorientation strategies can regain students' attention. This can include verbal phrases such as "1, 2, 3, eyes on me," physical actions such as hands raised, or sounds such as a timer. There is no one tool that works to reorient students in the classroom, and teachers need to identify what works for them. But shouting over students and getting frustrated when they are multitasking doesn't work.

> Teachers need to model concentration, focus, and stamina for students. When the adults around them look like they are multitasking, students think they can do the same.

CONNECTIONS

Do you model focused attention or multitasking?

_____
_____
_____
_____
_____
_____
_____
_____

How can you teach students about the myth of multitasking?

_____

_____

_____

_____

_____

_____

_____

Which reorientation strategies work in your classroom?

_____

_____

_____

_____

_____

_____

_____

_____

9. Constraints of Mental Effort and Working Memory

There are constraints on our biological learning system, our brain. In simple terms, there is only so much that our brains can do at a given time. Cognitive load theory explains that working memory has a limited capacity and that overloading it compromises learning. Cognitive load theory "assumes that knowledge can be divided into biologically primary knowledge that we have evolved to acquire and biologically secondary knowledge that is important for cultural reasons" (Sweller, 2011, p. 37). It's the secondary knowledge that is generally the focus of instruction.

> To reduce cognitive load for students, teachers can chunk information to make more efficient use of working memory.

At some point in every lesson, students approach their cognitive load. If the lessons exceed the cognitive load for students, they disengage and may even forget some of the previous learning. Importantly, all of us have limits to the amount of information we can process in our working memories and to how much mental effort we can exert. Cognitive load is influenced by several factors, including how much sleep we got, our interest level, our general wellness, and the structure of the information being presented.

To reduce cognitive load, teachers can chunk information to make more efficient use of working memory. After all, the goal of the learning experiences we design is to move concepts and skills from working memory into long-term memory, which we call learning. Exceeding students' working memory prevents this learning from happening. Essentially, chunking requires that the teacher break larger bits of information into smaller units and group these units in manageable ways. Yes, it's easier said than done. But when students disengage due to the constraints of their working memory and the mental effort required, it's worth looking at the way information has been structured and seeing if there are alternatives. Figure 8.5 identifies some of the major issues that should be considered regarding chunking.

Figure 8.5   Considerations When Chunking Information

Issue	Discussion
Prior Knowledge	We need to analyze what people already know about the topic, what they misunderstand, and what knowledge is missing. This lets us chunk according to their instructional needs. For example, if they have more prior knowledge, we can use larger chunks. If they have less prior knowledge, we should use smaller chunks. If they have misunderstandings or missing knowledge, we should include chunks that fix misunderstandings or offer missing knowledge.
Chunk Size	People cannot use prior knowledge to help them process what they are learning when they are new to a topic. Smaller chunks allow them to process a smaller amount at a time, which helps minimize the potential for overload. When people have more prior knowledge, we can meet their needs with larger chunks that offer targeted information for their specific needs.
Chunk Sequence	The sequence of chunks should be logical for the information offered and meet the instructional needs of the audience. For people new to a topic, for example, we often need to offer foundational information (such as terminology and underlying concepts) before more complex information.
Chunk Activities	To help people deeply process the content, we should ask questions and provide relevant practice and feedback and remembering activities. We should make sure that people can fill in missing knowledge and get answers to questions, get clarification, and fix misunderstandings.

Source: Shank (2018).

Note the recommendations about practice. Practice helps move information from working memory to long-term memory. The opposite of that is remembering. When we retrieve information from long-term memory and use it, learning is solidified. Retrieval practice, which was discussed in Module 7, helps reduce the demands on working memory.

PAUSE
AND
PONDER

What do you still want to learn about cognitive load theory?

_____

_____

_____

_____

_____

_____

_____

_____

_____

How can you chunk information for your students?

_____

_____

_____

_____

_____

_____

_____

_____

_____

_____

_____

We have presented these nine cognitive challenges in hopes that teachers learn to recognize the signs of each and then take action to re-engage students. Even better, these techniques provide a pathway to reducing disengagement in the first place. Of course, the goal is to teach students to drive their learning so that these challenges are increasingly rare in our classrooms. However, they do arise, and when we learn to recognize their signs and respond in ways that invite students back into learning, they are likely to learn more.

Challenges do arise, and when we learn to recognize their signs and respond in ways that invite students back into learning, the students are likely to learn more.

✏️ NOTE TO SELF

Questions	Notes and Reflections
How can I determine which cognitive barriers are impacting individual students in my classroom?	
What are some intentional actions I can take or experiences I can create to address students' mental mindset?	
What are some intentional actions I can take or experiences I can create to address students' metacognition and self-regulation?	
What are some intentional actions I can take or experiences I can create to address students' fear and mistrust?	
What are some intentional actions I can take or experiences I can create to address students with insufficient prior knowledge?	

Questions	Notes and Reflections
What are some intentional actions I can take or experiences I can create to address students' misconceptions?	
What are some intentional actions I can take or experiences I can create to address students with ineffective learning strategies?	
What are some intentional actions I can take or experiences I can create to address students' need for transfer of learning?	
What are some intentional actions I can take or experiences I can create to address students' selective attention?	
What are some intentional actions I can take or experiences I can create to address the constraints of mental effort and working memory?	

 TEACHER ACTIONS

Consider the following actions that reinforce or derail efforts to ensure that cognitive barriers to learning are recognized and addressed. We have included blank lines for you to add your ideas.

Teacher Actions That Reinforce an Understanding of the Cognitive Barriers to Learning	Teacher Actions That Derail an Understanding of the Cognitive Barriers to Learning
• Identifying a student's specific cognitive barrier to engagement • Selecting a teacher approach to match the cognitive barrier faced by the student • Modeling focus and concentration for students • Providing opportunities for near and far transfer of skills • Chunking information to make more efficient use of working memory so knowledge and skills can be transferred into long-term memory	• Assuming a student is disengaged because they don't care or they are not motivated • Giving feedback when it isn't wanted or the student isn't ready to receive it • Multitasking or modeling multitasking • Exceeding a student's working memory and not being aware of student cognitive load • Ignoring or not identifying common student misconceptions
_____	_____
_____	_____
_____	_____
_____	_____
_____	_____
_____	_____
_____	_____
_____	_____
_____	_____
_____	_____
_____	_____
_____	_____
_____	_____
_____	_____

CONCLUSION

Given our cognitive architecture, there are reasons that we disengage. In reality, It is pretty hard, if not impossible, to be endlessly "engaged" and drive your learning all the time. In some lessons, participation may be a starting point. But there are specific actions that teachers can take when students disengage, and there are experiences we can plan for students to increase the likelihood that they move from participation to driving. These lessons serve them well as they assume increased responsibility for their own learning and ideally become lifelong learners, which the business world describes as "the ongoing, voluntary, and self-motivated pursuit of knowledge for either personal or professional reasons" (Roman-Cohen, 2020). And wouldn't we all be proud if we had a hand in helping students accomplish that?

> There are specific actions that teachers can take when students disengage, and there are experiences we can plan for students to increase the likelihood that they move from participation to driving.

NOTES

_____
_____
_____
_____
_____
_____
_____
_____
_____
_____
_____
_____
_____
_____
_____
_____
_____
_____
_____
_____
_____
_____

RETELLING PYRAMID

Create a pyramid of words, using the following prompts, that provides summarizing information. You're more likely to remember this information if you share with a peer.

1. One word that conveys an important topic in this module

2. Two words for teacher approaches to cognitive barriers to engagement

3. Three words for actions you can take based on this module

4. Four words that are key to your understanding

5. Five words that convey a goal you have based on this module

_____

_____   _____

_____   _____   _____

_____   _____   _____   _____

_____   _____   _____   _____   _____

Revisit the Text Impression summary you developed at the beginning of this module, and compare it to your current level of understanding. Where did your learning deepen?

_____

_____

_____

_____

_____

_____

_____

_____

_____

_____

_____

_____

_____

Using the traffic light scale, with red being not confident, yellow being somewhat confident, and green indicating very confident, how confident are you in your ability to

- Recognize signs of disrupting, withdrawing, and avoiding learning?

- Describe nine cognitive barriers to learning?

- Identify actions to take when cognitive barriers arise?

REFERENCES

Absolum, M., Flockton, L., Hattie, J., Hipkins, R., & Reid, I. (2009). *Directions for assessment in New Zealand (DANZ): Developing students' assessment capabilities.* New Zealand Ministry of Education.

Adesope, O. O., Trevisan, D. A., & Sundararajan, N. (2017). Rethinking the use of tests: A meta-analysis of practice testing. *Review of Educational Research, 87*(3), 659–701.

Agarwal, P. K., Nunes, L. D., & Blunt, J. R. (2021). Retrieval practice consistently benefits student learning: A systematic review of applied research in schools and classrooms. *Educational Psychology Review, 33,* 1409–1453.

Alegre-Ansuategui, F. J., Moliner, L., Lorenzo, G., & Maroto, A. (2017). Peer tutoring and academic achievement in mathematics: A meta-analysis. *Eurasia Journal of Mathematics, Science and Technology Education, 14,* 337–354.

Alexander, K. (2017). *The playbook: 52 rules to aim, shoot, and score in this game called life.* HMH Books for Young Readers.

Almarode, J., Fisher, D., Thunder, K., & Frey, N. (2021). *The success criteria playbook: A hands-on guide to making learning visible and measurable.* Corwin.

Almeda, V., Baker, R., & Corbett, A. (2017). Help avoidance: When students should seek help, and the consequences of failing to do so. *Teachers College Record, 119*(3), 1–24.

Andrade, H. L. (2019). A critical review of research on student self-assessment. *Frontiers in Education, 4.* https://doi.org/10.3389/feduc.2019.00087

Bandura, A. (1997). *Self-efficacy: The exercise of control.* W. H. Freeman.

Barshay, J. (2011). How a "tech break" can help students refocus. *The Hechinger Report.* https://hechingerreport.org/how-a-tech-break-can-help-students-refocus/

Baumann, J. F., Jones, L. A., & Seifert-Kessell, N. (1993). Using think alouds to enhance children's comprehension monitoring abilities. *The Reading Teacher, 47,* 184–193.

Berger, R., Rugen, L., & Woodfin, L. (2014). *Leaders of their own learning: Transforming schools through student-engaged assessment.* Jossey-Bass.

Berry, A. (2022). *Reimagining student engagement: From disrupting to driving.* Corwin.

Berry, A. (2020). Disrupting to driving: Exploring upper primary teachers' perspectives on student engagement. *Teachers and Teaching, 26*(2), 145–165.

Bong, M. (2013). Self-efficacy. In J. Hattie & E. M. Anderman (Eds.), *International guide to student achievement* (pp. 64–66). Routledge.

Brown, G. T. L., & Harris, L. R. (2014). The future of self-assessment in classroom practice: Reframing self-assessment as a core competency. *Frontline Learning Research, 3,* 22–30.

Butler, R. (1998). Determinants of help seeking: Relations between perceived reasons for classroom help-avoidance and help-seeking behaviors in an experimental context. *Journal of Educational Psychology, 90,* 630–643.

Butler, R., & Shibaz, L. (2014). Striving to connect and striving to learn: Influences of relational and mastery goals for teaching on teacher behaviors and student interest and help seeking. *International Journal of Educational Research, 65,* 41–53.

Caprara, G., Fida, R., Vecchione, M., Del Bove, G., Vecchio, G., Barabaranelli, C., & Bandura, A. (2008). Longitudinal analysis of the role of perceived self-efficacy for self-regulatory learning in academic continuance an achievement. *Journal of Educational Psychology, 100*(3), 525–534.

Carless, D., & Boud, D. (2018). The development of student feedback literacy: Enabling uptake of feedback. *Assessment & Evaluation in Higher Education, 43*(8), 1315–1325, DOI: 10.1080/02602938.2018.1463354

Carless, D., & Winstone, N. (2023). Teacher feedback literacy and its interplay with student feedback literacy. *Teaching in Higher Education, 28*(1), 150–163.

Chew, S. L., & Cerbin, W. J. (2021). The cognitive challenges of effective teaching. *The Journal of Economic Education, 52*(1), 17–40. https://doi.org/10.1080/00220485.2020.1845266

Childs, J., & Lofton, R. (2021). Masking attendance: How education policy distracts from the wicked problem(s) of chronic absenteeism. *Educational Policy, 35*(2), 213–234.

Claxton, G., & Lucas, B. (2016). The hole in the heart of education (and the role of psychology in addressing it). *The Psychology of Education Review, 40*(1), 4–12.

Conley, D. T., & French, E. M. (2014). Student ownership of learning as a key component of college readiness. *American Behavioral Scientist, 58*(8), 1018–1034.

Cook, J., & Lewandowsky, S. (2011). *The debunking handbook.* University of Queensland.

Crenshaw, D. (2008). *The myth of multitasking: How "doing it all" gets nothing done.* Jossey-Bass.

Davey, B. (1983). Thinking aloud—Modeling the cognitive processes of reading comprehension. *Journal of Reading, 27*, 44–47.

Deans for Impact. (2016). *Practice with purpose: The emerging science of teacher expertise.* Author.

Dewey, J. (1933). *How we think: A restatement of the relation of reflective thinking to the educative process.* Henry Regnery.

Duffelmeyer, F. (1994). Effective anticipation guide statements for learning from expository prose. *Journal of Reading, 37*, 452–455.

Dweck, C. S. (2016). Praise the effort, not the outcome? Think again. *TES: Times Educational Supplement, 5182*, 38–39.

Eccles, J., & Wang, M. T. (2012). So what is student engagement anyway? In S. L. Christenson, A. L. Reschly, & C. Wylie (Eds.), *Handbook of research on student engagement* (pp. 133–145). Springer Science.

Elhusseini, S. A., Tischner, C. M., Aspiranti, K. B., & Fedewa, A. L. (2022). A quantitative review of the effects of self-regulation interventions on primary and secondary student academic achievement. *Metacognition & Learning, 17*(3), 1117–1139.

Ericsson, A., & Pool, R. (2016). *Peak: Secrets from the new science of expertise.* Houghton Mifflin Harcourt.

Ericsson, K. A., Krampe, R. T., & Tesch-Römer, C. (1993). The role of deliberate practice in the acquisition of expert performance. *Psychological Review, 100*, 363–406.

Fearn, L., & Farnan, N. (2001). *Interactions: Teaching writing and the language arts.* Houghton Mifflin.

Fendick, F. (1990). *The correlation between teacher clarity of communication and student achievement gain: A meta-analysis* [Unpublished doctoral dissertation]. University of Florida, Gainesville.

Finn, A. N., Schrodt, P., Witt, P. L., Elledge, N., Jernberg, K. A., & Larson, L. M. (2009). A meta-analytical review of teacher credibility and its associations with teacher behaviors and student outcomes. *Communication Education, 58*(4), 516–537.

Fisher, D., & Frey, N. (2021). *Better learning through structured teaching: A framework for the gradual release of responsibility* (3rd ed.). ASCD.

Fisher, D., & Frey, N. (2007). *Scaffolded writing instruction.* Scholastic.

Fisher, D., Frey, N., Bustamante, V., & Hattie, J. (2021). *The assessment playbook for distance and blended learning: Measuring student learning in any setting.* Corwin.

Fisher, D., Frey, N., Hattie, J., & Flories, K. T. (2018). *Becoming an assessment-capable visible learner, grades 6-12, level 1: Learner's notebook.* Corwin.

Fisher, D., Frey, N., Smith, D., & Hattie, J. (2021). *Rebound: A playbook for rebuilding agency, accelerating learning recovery, and rethinking schools.* Corwin.

Fredricks, J. A., Blumenfeld, P., & Paris, A. H. (2004). School engagement: Potential of the concept, state of the evidence. *Review of Educational Research, 74*(1), 59–109.

Frey, N., Fisher, D., & Almarode, A. (2023). *How scaffolding works: A playbook for supporting and releasing responsibility to students.* Corwin.

Frey, N., Fisher, D., & Almarode, J. (2021). *How tutoring works: Six steps to grow motivation and accelerate student learning.* Corwin.

Frey, N., Fisher, D., & Hattie, J. (2018). Developing "assessment capable" learners. *Educational Leadership, 75*(5), 46–51.

Fuchs, D., Fuchs, L., & Burish, P. (2000). Peer-assisted learning strategies: An evidence-based practice to promote reading achievement. *Learning Disabilities Research and Practice, 15*(2), 85–91.

Fuchs, L. S., Fuchs, D., & Kazdan, S. (1999). Effects of peer-assisted learning strategies on high school students with serious reading problems. *Remedial and Special Education, 20*(5), 309–318.

Gee, J. P. (2014). *An introduction to discourse analysis: Theory and mind.* Routledge.

Gonzalez, J. (2014). Know your terms: Holistic, analytic, and single-point rubrics. *Cult of Pedagogy.* www.cultofpedagogy.com/holistic-analytic-single-point-rubrics

Gross-Loh, C. (2016, December 16). How praise became a consolation prize. *The Atlantic.* https://www.theatlantic.com/education/archive/2016/12/how-praise-became-a-consolation-prize/510845

Ha Dinh, T. T., Bonner, A., Clark, R., Ramsbotham, J., & Hines, S. (2016). The effectiveness of the teach-back method on adherence and self-management in health education for people with chronic disease: A systematic review. *JBI Database of Systematic Reviews and Implementation, 14*(1), 210–247.

Haddix, M. P. (2000). *Among the hidden.* Simon & Schuster.

Hanson, D. (2017, September 27). Fostering a growth mindset: Viewing constructive criticism as helpful feedback. *Crafting Connections* [Blog]. https://www.crafting-connections.com/2017/09/fostering-growth-mindset-viewing.html?m=1&epik=dj0yJnU9cnMxaktQVmlUNVVGZmstS1pzQlhZWHJsdWFtYXg4MW8mcD0wJm49VjhBTkwzREh3a05CNWJ5NWtlcjkydyZ0PUFBQUFBR092SjFJ

Hattie, J. (2023). *Visible learning: The sequel.* Routledge.

Hattie, J. (2012). *Visible learning for teachers: Maximizing impact on learning.* Routledge.

Hattie, J. (2009). *Visible learning: A synthesis of over 800 meta-analyses relating to achievement.* Routledge.

Hattie, J., & Donoghue, G. M. (2016). Learning strategies: A synthesis and conceptual model. *Science of Learning, 1.* https://doi.org/10.1038/npjscilearn.2016.13

Hattie, J., Fisher, D., Frey, N., & Clarke, S. (2021). *Collective student efficacy: Developing independent and inter-dependent learners.* Corwin.

Hattie, J., & Timperley, H. (2007). The power of feedback. *Review of Educational Research, 77*(1), 81–112.

Hoover, J. J., & Patton, P. R. (1995). *Teaching students with learning problems to use study skills: A teacher's guide.* Pro-Ed.

Jacobson, J., Thrope, L., Fisher, D., Lapp, D., Frey, N., & Flood, J. (2001). Cross age tutoring: A literacy improvement approach for struggling adolescent readers. *Journal of Adolescent and Adult Literacy, 44,* 528–536.

Joseph, L. M., Alber-Morgan, S., Cullen, J., & Rouse, C. (2016). The effects of self-questioning on reading comprehension: A literature review. *Reading & Writing Quarterly, 32*(2), 152–173.

Kapur, M. (2016). Examining productive failure, productive success, unproductive failure, and unproductive success in learning. *Educational Psychologist, 51*(2), 289–299.

Ketonen, L., Nieminen, P., & Hähkiöniemi, M. (2020). The development of secondary students' feedback literacy: Peer assessment as an intervention. *The Journal of Educational Research, 113*(6), 407–417.

King, A. (1992). Facilitating elaborative learning through guided student-generated questioning. *Educational Psychologist, 27*(11), 111–126.

Kowalski, P., & Taylor, A. K. (2017). Reducing students' misconceptions with refutational teaching: For long-term retention, verbal ability matters. *Journal of the Scholarship of Teaching and Learning in Psychology, 3*(2), 90–100.

Krupp, A. (2017, June 7). How do you know you've learned something? *Sensemaking.* https:// alexkrupp.typepad.com/sensemaking/2007/06/how_do_you_know.html

LaBerge, D., & Samuels, S. J. (1974). Toward a theory of automatic information processing in reading. *Cognitive Psychology, 6*(2), 293–323.

Lassiter, C., Fisher, D., Frey, N., & Smith, D. (2022). *How leadership works: A playbook for instructional leaders.* Corwin.

Levine, E. (2007). *Henry's freedom box: A true story from the underground railroad.* Scholastic.

Littman, S. D. (2016). *Backlash.* Scholastic.

McGinley, W. J., & Denner, P. R. (1987). Story impressions: A prereading/writing activity. *Journal of Reading, 31*(3), 248–253.

Maheady, L., Harper, G. F., & Mallette, B. (2001). Peer-mediated instruction and interventions and students with mild disabilities. *Remedial and Special Education, 22,* 4–15.

Mandouit, L., & Hattie, J. (2023). Revisiting "The Power of Feedback" from the perspective of the learner. *Learning and Instruction, 84*(101718). https://doi.org/10.1016/j .learninstruc.2022.101718

Martin, A. J. (2013). Goal orientation. In J. Hattie & E. M. Anderman (Eds.), *International guide to student achievement* (pp. 353–355). Routledge.

Martin, A. J., Marsh, H. W., & Debus, R. L. (2003). Self-handicapping and defensive pessimism: A model of self-protection from a longitudinal perspective. *Contemporary Educational Psychology, 28*(1), 1–36.

Moliner, L., & Alegre, F. (2020). Effects of peer tutoring on middle school students' mathematics self-concepts. *PLOS ONE, 15*(4), e0231410. https://doi.org/10.1371/journal.pone.0231410

Morrow, L. M. (1985). Retelling stories: A strategy for improving young children's comprehension, concept of story structure, and oral language complexity. *The Elementary School Journal, 85*(5), 647–661.

Nuthall, G. (2007). *The hidden lives of learners.* NZCER Press.

Palacio, R. J. (2012). *Wonder.* Alfred A. Knopf.

Palincsar, A. S., & Brown, A. (1984). Reciprocal teaching of comprehension-fostering and comprehension-monitoring activities. *Cognition and Instruction, 1*(2), 117–175.

Pauk, W. (1962). *How to study in college.* Houghton Mifflin.

Priniski, S. J., Hecht, C. A., & Harackiewicz, J. M. (2018). Making learning personally meaningful: A new framework for relevance research. *Journal of Experimental Education, 86,* 11–29.

Qin, W., Kingston, H. C., & Kim, J. S. (2019). What does retelling "tell" about children's reading proficiency? *First Language, 39*(2), 177–199.

Reinholz, D. L. (2015). Peer-assisted reflection: A design-based intervention for improving success in calculus. *International Journal of Research in Undergraduate Mathematics Education, 1,* 234–267.

Reynolds, J. (2016). *Ghost.* Antheneum.

Roman-Cohen, T. (2020). *Follow these four simple steps to become a lifelong learner.* https:// www.mba.com/business-school-and-careers/career-possibilities/follow-these-four-sim ple-steps-to-become -a-lifelong-learner

Sadler, P. M., & Good, E. (2006). The impact of self- and peer-grading on student learning. *Educational Assessment, 11*(1), 1–31.

Sanchez, C. E., Atkinson, K. M., Koenka, A. C., Moshontz, H., & Cooper, H. (2017). Self-grading and peer-grading for formative and summative assessments in 3rd through 12th grade classrooms: A meta-analysis. *Journal of Educational Psychology, 109*(8), 1049–1066.

Schoenfeld, A. H. (1992). Learning to think mathematically: Problem-solving, metacognition, and sense-making in mathematics. In D. Grouws (Ed.), *Handbook for research in mathematics teaching and learning* (pp. 334–370). Macmillan.

Shank, P. (2018). What research tells us about chunking content. *eLearning Industry.* https://elearningindustry.com/chunking-content-what-research-tells-us

Sotola, L. K., & Crede, M. (2021). Regarding class quizzes: A meta-analytic synthesis of studies on the relationship between frequent low-stakes testing and class performance. *Educational Psychology Review, 33*(2), 407–426.

Stahl, N. A., King, J. R., & Henk, W. A. (1991). Enhancing students' notetaking through training and evaluation. *Journal of Reading, 34*, 614–622.

Sutton, S. (2012). Conceptualizing feedback literacy: Knowing, being, and acting. *Innovations in Education and Teaching International, 49*(1), 31–40, DOI: 10.1080/14703297.2012.647781

Sweller, J. (2011). Cognitive load theory. In J. P. Mestre & B. H. Ross (Eds.), *Psychology of learning and motivation* (Vol. 55, pp. 37–76). Academic Press.

Taggart, A. R., & Laughlin, M. (2017). Affect matters: When writing feedback leads to negative feeling. *International Journal Scholarship in Teaching and Learning, 11*(2). https://doi.org/10.20429/ijsotl.2017.110213

Telgemeier, R. (2010). *Smile.* Scholastic Graphix.

Voerman, L. A., Meijer, P., Korthagen, F., & Simons, R. P. (2012). Types and frequencies of feedback interventions in classroom interaction in secondary education. *Teaching & Teacher Education, 28*(8), 1107–1115.

Werft, S. (2019, May 15). *How do you know you've learned something?* https://www.linkedin.com/pulse/how-do-you-know-youve-learned-something-stjepan-werft/

Wisniewski, B., Zierer, K., & Hattie, J. (2020). The power of feedback revisited: A meta-analysis of educational feedback research. *Frontiers in Psychology, 10*, 3087. https://doi.org/10.3389/fpsyg.2019.03087

Zumbrunn, S., Ekholm, E., Stringer, J. S., McKnight, K. M., & DeBusk-Lane, M. D. (2017). Student experiences with writing: Taking the temperature of the classroom. *The Reading Teacher, 70*(6), 667–677.

Zumbrunn, S., Marrs, S., & Mewborn, C. (2016). Toward a better understanding of student perceptions of writing feedback: A mixed methods study. *Reading & Writing, 29*(2), 349–370.

INDEX

A SAGE Publishing Company

Helping educators make the greatest impact

CORWIN HAS ONE MISSION: to enhance education through intentional professional learning.

We build long-term relationships with our authors, educators, clients, and associations who partner with us to develop and continuously improve the best evidence-based practices that establish and support lifelong learning.

CORWIN Fisher & Frey

 Every student deserves a great teacher—
not by chance, but by design.

Read more from Fisher & Frey

Learn to create a culture of feedback in your classroom with the latest research on teaching, engagement, and assessment with this concise and interactive playbook.

Rich with resources that support the process of parlaying scientific findings into classroom practice, this playbook offers all the moves teachers need to design learning experiences that work for all students.

This easy-to-use playbook prompts educators to clarify, articulate, and actualize instructional leadership goals with the aim of delivering on the promise of equity and excellence for all.

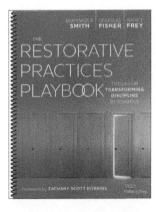

Transform negative behavior into a teachable moment at your school, utilizing restorative practices that are grounded in relationships and a commitment to the well-being of others.

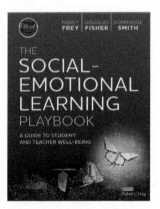

This interactive playbook provides the language, moves, and evidence-based advice you need to nurture social and emotional learning in yourself, your students, and your school.

Harnessing decades of Visible Learning® research, this easy-to-read, eye-opening guide details the six essential components of effective tutoring.

To order your copies, visit corwin.com/FisherandFrey